SOCIOLOGY
THE STUDY OF SOCIAL SYSTEMS

SOCIOLOGY

THE STUDY OF SOCIAL SYSTEMS

BY

G. DUNCAN MITCHELL, M.B.E., B.Sc.(Econ.)

PROFESSOR OF SOCIOLOGY, UNIVERSITY OF EXETER

Author of *A Hundred Years of Sociology*
and Editor of *A Dictionary of Sociology*

UNIVERSITY TUTORIAL PRESS LTD

9-10 GREAT SUTTON STREET, LONDON, E.C.1

Published 1959
Reprinted 1960, 1963
Reprinted (with minor additions) 1966
Reprinted 1967
Second Edition 1970

ISBN: 0 7231 0520 0

PRINTED IN GREAT BRITAIN BY UNIVERSITY TUTORIAL PRESS LTD
FOXTON, NEAR CAMBRIDGE

PREFACE TO THE FIRST EDITION

THIS book is about human society. Of any social phenomenon there are a number of fundamental questions which we may ask. Thus we may ask: how did it come to be what it is? This is fundamentally an historical question. We may also ask: what is the relationship of this contemporary phenomenon to others? This I would call a sociological question. Of course we may instead ask: why does this person behave in the way he does? And this is basically a psychological question. To fully understand human society we need to ask all three kinds of questions, for history, sociology, and psychology are not alternatives; they are complementary. The contribution of this book is a partial one, for it takes its point of departure from the second kind of question. It must not, however, be supposed that historians do not treat their material sociologically, for some do, nor that sociologists eschew history, for some of the most imposing achievements have been in the field of historical sociology. Moreover, numerous sociological studies have also been psychological ones too. These distinctions between fundamental kinds of questions are analytical distinctions.

What I have attempted to do in this work is to outline concisely the hard core of a distinguishable discipline and to do so in terms of both subject and method. For this purpose I define sociology as a descriptive and analytical discipline concerned with the structural aspects of human society. In particular I emphasise the idea of society as a social system or a number of social systems. Many sociologists, however, are also interested in making use of the comparative method, and in so far as this may be used, sociology tries to be a generalising discipline. Whilst the main intention of this book is to provide a useful introduction to those undertaking the academic study of sociology, it is hoped that it will have a wider appeal. This is a reasonable hope because, in as much as it is both an analytical and generalising discipline, sociology should have some practical application. People concerned with practical social matters, such as the administrator, the social worker, and the educationist should find in this discipline much to help them. Such people as these are the products of their society, but they also are the instruments whereby changes are brought about in it. The study of sociology may help them to understand more fully the implications of their actions: be they altering the working relationships of their employees, helping a problem-family to help itself, or selecting children for different types of education and training. The subject has been dealt with in three parts. The first part briefly outlines the history of sociology from the writer's own perspective, and proffers an orientation together with a number of useful analytical concepts and an illustration of their use. The second and third parts treat respectively the relatively simple non-literate society and the complex urban industrial society. As regards the latter most of the references made to investigations and examples are to modern Britain; it is hoped thereby to redress the balance to some extent, for in respect to textbooks there is at present a heavy weighting in favour of America.

This work has largely arisen out of my experiences in teaching sociology in the Universities of Liverpool, Birmingham, Oxford, and Exeter. What merits it may possess are owed chiefly to my teachers, colleagues, and students. In particular I take this opportunity to acknowledge my debt to Professor E. A. Shils, of the University of Chicago, who originally stimulated my interest in the subject and wisely directed my thoughts; to Dr Joséphine Klein and Dr Michael Beesley, of the University of Birmingham, for many helpful discussions of theoretical problems; to my present colleagues: Professor D. J. O'Connor, who gave me the notion of writing this book and who kindly read the proofs, Miss M. P. Callard, who gave me assistance with the statistical material in Chapter IX, Miss U. M. Cormack, with whom I have had useful discussions on the relevance of sociology to social work, and especially to Dr Margaret Hewitt, who has read the entire manuscript, made several valuable suggestions, and whose advice and criticisms I gratefully acknowledge. I wish also to express my appreciation to Miss M. Gardiner for secretarial assistance during a particularly busy period. I am indebted to the following for permission to reproduce quotations or diagrams from works individually described in the Chapter Bibliographies: Messrs Cohen and West Ltd, and Professor E. E. Evans-Pritchard, the Clarendon Press, Messrs Routledge and Kegan Paul Ltd, the Oxford University Press (on behalf of the International African Institute), the Harvard University Press, Messrs Macmillan and Co. Ltd, and the Macmillan Company, New York, Messrs Weidenfeld and Nicolson Ltd, and the Royal Anthropological Institute of Great Britain and Ireland.

                                                    DUNCAN MITCHELL.
University of Exeter.

PREFACE TO THE SECOND EDITION

It is now over a decade since this small introductory book on Sociology appeared and, although it is still widely used, a revision has long been overdue.

When it was originally conceived, the idea of presenting the subject in terms of a contrast of the simple and complex types of societies had perhaps more obvious contemporary relevance than it does to-day. But if it was difficult in the 1950s to find for investigation a traditional, simple, non-literate society uncontaminated by the influence of western ideas and by modern industry and commerce, it may well be held that now it is quite impossible. Yet the essence of sociology lies in making comparisons between types of societies and if the modern student tends rather to jib at anything other than the contemporary scene it is the teacher's task to show him the intellectual advantages that flow from a comparative examination of types of societies both past and present. In short, the justification for the approach made in this introductory book remains what it was.

It has not been possible to make a complete revision of the whole book but there has been some revision and extension of Chapter I, a slight modification in Chapter IV, and both Chapters IX and X have been completely re-written and brought up to date, as have also the Bibliographies at the end of these and other chapters.

G. D. M.

Exeter.

CONTENTS

PART I

INTRODUCTION TO THE HISTORY AND THEORY OF SOCIOLOGY

PART II

THE PRINCIPAL SOCIAL INSTITUTIONS OF THE SIMPLE SOCIETY

PART III

SYSTEMATIC ANALYSIS OF THE COMPLEX SOCIETY

PART I
INTRODUCTION TO THE HISTORY AND THEORY OF SOCIOLOGY

SOCIOLOGY

THE STUDY OF SOCIAL SYSTEMS

CHAPTER I

THE ORIGINS AND DEVELOPMENT OF SOCIOLOGY

Sociology may be said to be very largely a child of *The Enlightenment*. When Denis Diderot and Jean D'Alembert edited the famous Encyclopaedia in France, published between 1751 and 1780, they were successful in securing the collaboration of some of the best minds in Europe. Their object was to make a synthesis of all available knowledge, and in doing so to be unprejudiced, objective, and non-partisan. They were guided by a vision of a unified European culture based on commonly accepted methods of thought; hence their abandonment of many traditional but conflicting theological and philosophical notions, their interest in scientific method, and their endeavour to bring into close relationship both humanism and science. Here, then, we have one example of the intellectual labours of European thinkers whose thought contributed to the ferment of ideas described by this historical term—*The Enlightenment*. Famous men of ideas in this period were many; among them were Montesquieu, De Maistre, Condorcet, Saint Simon, and Comte in France; Lessing, von Herder, and Hegel in Germany; and Locke, Hume, Adam Ferguson, and Jeremy Bentham in Britain. If we take a brief look at a few of them and at the same time bear in mind the kind of social background against which they thought and wrote, we shall begin to see how sociology as a distinctive discipline came into being.

Comte on the Development of Society

The word *sociology* appeared first in the fourth volume of a book entitled *Cours de philosophie positive* by Auguste Comte (1798-1857), which he published in 1839. It is convenient to begin with a review of Comte's thought, not because he invented the subject, which we can hardly say he did, but because he was an influential writer to whom later sociologists like Durkheim, Spencer, Hobhouse, and Radcliffe-Brown in their several ways owed much. He was not a particularly original thinker. Indeed, many of his ideas he took from others. It is advisable, therefore, to consider some of these people and also the social circumstances of his time.

Several thinkers had entertained the idea that the history of mankind was governed by an order and that it was possible to discern its lawful nature. Comte was fascinated by this idea of the natural development of society, but in addition he obtained from Condorcet (1743-94) the notion that this evolution of society is attended by progress. He thought that he could discern three stages of development: three stages of intellectual development in the first place, but each corresponding to three stages of social development. His famous Law of the Three Stages had previously been stated in rudimentary form by both R. J. Turgot (1727-81) and Saint Simon (1760-1825), but Comte developed it and rendered it popular. In short, he argued that every branch of human knowledge must pass through three successive stages of theoretical development: the theological or fictive, the metaphysical or abstract, and the scientific or positive stages.

The basis of Comte's argument is inductive. He shows how the history of thought is adequately described by this law, and asserts that there are no known cases of the order of development being reversed. He points out that primitive man interprets and observes in terms of his experience, and that this leads him to humanise and personalise natural phenomena so that natural objects, like mountains and streams, are thought of as possessing powers of will and consciousness and, indeed, may be possessed by spirits. From this, Comte says, man came to depend in his thinking on the existence of a power or powers not his own, and which it was necessary to know in order to make sense of the world he lived in and find it meaningful. This is the first stage of intellectual development, but even so from the beginning there was something of the positive science that he advocated, for man had always noted certain natural regularities not only with regard to inanimate objects but with respect to animate ones, indeed to human beings, and this developed as the second stage was reached. This was the metaphysical stage, not very different from the first except that personal deities and spirits gave way to the use of abstractions like essences and forces. But this was a more critical stage, and because it was critical and also self-critical it soon passed into the third and positive stage where man observes nature and humanity objectively and dispassionately, not trying to explain phenomena in terms of their origins or the ends they serve, but seeking to discern laws of co-existence and succession. If, for example, there is never rainfall except when clouds gather in the sky, then here we have a co-existence. We are not concerned, Comte would say, with why rain falls or clouds gather, except in so far as we can note the uniformity; when rain falls there are clouds in the sky and the latter precede the former.

Comte then tries to establish a parallel development of human society from a stage which may be called militarism to one he calls juristic or legal, and this in turn to an industrial stage. Militarism, he argued, was necessary for the development of primitive social groups; it helped instil discipline and bound them together in coherent order. Moreover, there was a link between the theological and the military stages in that military leaders relied on theological backing —men are held together more strongly and fight the better when serving supernatural ends. The juristic or legal stage of social development acted as a solvent for the first stage. Here wars are more defensive and internal order rests more on legal and constitutional arrangements than upon force and fear. The links with the metaphysical or abstract stage are not difficult to see; and again the link between science and industrial development is obvious.

Now all this description of the history of human thought and social life seems to us to-day a very crude interpretation, but we may appreciate its plausibility in Comte's time if we consider the social events of the day, for this was a period when the benefits of industrialisation were becoming apparent, whilst behind lay the discredited attempts to found a unified Europe by military force and the apparent ruination of the Catholic Church in France. The future, it seemed, was to be dominated by economic expansion, by peace among the nations, and by a growing body of commonly accepted scientific knowledge. Above all, there would be internal order, and here the wish was father to the thought, for the Revolution had threatened and destroyed the security of many people.

Comte passionately believed that there could be stability within and peace without, that there could be plenty for all, and, indeed, a new world if the positive spirit prevailed and scientists were in control; science for Comte included sociology, which he saw as the crown of intellectual achievement. In fact, the development of sociology was of paramount importance, for it would react back on the other sciences and humanise them, pointing to their true function of benefiting humanity. This was not merely a hopeful dream to Comte, for he held it to be inevitable. He saw himself standing at the beginning of a new era for which he, as an instrument of nature, had provided the blue-print. His plan was a product of the hope and intellectual excitement of *The Enlightenment*, but it was also a product of the fear and insecurity of the Revolution and the Napoleonic wars. It was a scheme for scientific social development and it influenced many people; in this his claim to have founded sociology may be said to have some justification.

German Ideas of History

A not altogether dissimilar notion about the course of human history developing according to a lawful order was entertained by writers in Germany. It gained currency largely as a result of a book by Lessing, *Education of the Human Race*, in which the author applied the concept of development to the history of religion. This conception was taken up by another German writer, von Herder, and extended to the whole life of man. It seemed to him that everything grows and develops, and in his *Ideas for the philosophy of the history of mankind*, which appeared toward the end of the eighteenth century, he attempted to bring the whole course of human development under the conception of a unitary process.

This particular tradition came to efflorescence in the work of Hegel, who saw a single principle, the dialectic, as the key to our understanding of all history, and not only history but many other problems of philosophy. Yet it was history especially that for Hegel could be interpreted in terms of a dialectical law of development; a development in which the contradictions and oppositions in the world are not denied and annulled but are combined in a richer whole which gives them each a relative validity. In development, he argued, there are three stages: thesis, antithesis, and synthesis; and synthesis includes both the thesis and the antithesis. Persons do not achieve individuality except in relation to other persons, the state does not achieve individuality except in relation to other states, thesis interacts with its antithesis to become a synthesis. Conflict is endemic to development. For Hegel history is progress in the consciousness of a rational freedom, and he traces it from the Orient through Greek civilisation to Rome with its development of law and finally to the emergent Europe in which he thought the Germanic peoples were to play so large a part. Here is developed the nation-state, powerful, stable, and productive, which he believed the developed individual in his freedom has the privilege of choosing to serve.

Now why are we concerned with this particular tradition, which is both rather fanciful and very Teutonic and really has no very direct bearing on modern sociology? The reason is that it is part and parcel of the *historicist* tradition which we have seen in Comte, and most particularly it is the tradition of thought which culminated in the work of Karl Marx (1818-83), for Marx was an Hegelian; he accepted Hegel's metaphysic, what the latter called his logic or dialectical principle, and he also applied it to history, although in a rather different way from his master, and applied it with considerable effect. Indeed, modern sociology owes to Marx as much as, perhaps more than, it does to Comte.

Marx on Capitalism and Social Classes

When we speak of *historicism* we refer to the attempt to discern a law governing social development. Sometimes the term *philosophy of history* is used instead to denote this endeavour; indeed, Hegel's work was entitled *Lectures on the Philosophy of History*, but this term is also often used to refer to the critical examination of the method used by historians. Now whilst Hegel was concerned to point to the conflicts between nation-states, Marx saw the significant conflict to be between classes. Believing with Hegel that entities do not exist by themselves, but are distinguishable only in terms of their contraries, he held that a social phenomenon like a class existed only because it was distinguishable from another class with which it was in a state of conflict. Feudal lord and serf were each members of opposing classes, so were guild-master and journeyman. He saw that societies at different times have different and sometimes complex patterns of classes, but he also saw that in his own day the structure of classes was being simplified and

6 SOCIOLOGY

that the nature of social development was such as to bring into existence only two classes: the *bourgeoisie* and the *proletariat*. Consider, for example, this passage from the Communist Manifesto: *

"Of all the classes that stand face to face with the bourgeoisie today, the proletariat alone is a really revolutionary class. The other classes decay and finally disappear in the face of modern industry; the proletariat is its special and essential product.

"The lower middle class, the small manufacturer, the shopkeeper, the artisan, the peasant, all these fight against the bourgeoisie, to save from extinction their existence as fractions of the middle class. They are therefore not revolutionary, but conservative. Nay more, they are reactionary, for they try to roll back the wheel of history. If by chance they are revolutionary, they are so only in view of their impending transfer into the proletariat; they thus defend not their present, but their future interests, they desert their own standpoint to place themselves at that of the proletariat." (p. 42.)

For Marx the class struggle was the key to our understanding of history, and, what is more, he believed that a proper understanding of history would enable us to predict in just the same way as a natural scientist, once he understands the lawful order, is able to say that given such and such conditions a certain process will occur. Here again, we have an attempt to wed science and humanism, for Marx wanted not only to predict the future, but to ensure that the future held in store a better social order than the one he knew. Industrialisation, particularly in England, had brought many evils, as his friend Frederick Engels had outlined in his book, *The Conditions of the Working-Class in England in 1844.*† To Marx the capitalist social order was hateful, and he eagerly looked forward to its dissolution and to the revolution which would usher in the Dictatorship of the Proletariat, a temporary stage, and ultimately the classless society where each would receive according to his need as each would give according to his ability. Apart from the Communist Manifesto, which gives a succinct summary of the

* First published in German in 1848, in English in 1850; see *Karl Marx and Frederick Engels: Selected Works*, Vol. I, 1951.
† First published in German in 1845, in English in 1885.

argument, it is nowhere very fully stated, although it is implied in much that Marx wrote of an historical nature, such as *The Eighteenth Brumaire of Louis Bonaparte*, and is also included in his major work, *Capital*.

Marx's work may be regarded as falling into two divisions: on the one hand, there is his economic interpretation of history, sometimes misleadingly called the materialist interpretation of history,* and on the other hand there is his sociological theory of classes. What is important in the former from a sociologist's viewpoint is what he had to say about the relationship between beliefs, ideas, and thought, what he termed the superstructure of society, and the mode of production or the kind of economic arrangements that characterise a society at any one period of its history. It is important because Marx held that the study of what people have thought and believed is much less fruitful than the study of economic relationships. Indeed, he maintained that the relationship a person has to the economic arrangements of society conditions his beliefs and ideas about that society, and there is a famous passage in which he describes his views very clearly on this subject:

"In the social production of their life, men enter into definite relations that are indispensable and independent of their will, relations of production which correspond to a definite stage of development of their material productive forces. The sum total of these relations of production constitutes the economic structure of society, the real foundation, on which rises a legal and political superstructure and to which correspond definite forms of social consciousness. The mode of production of material life conditions the social, political, and intellectual life process in general. It is not the consciousness of men that determines their being, but, on the contrary, their social being that determines their consciousness".†

* Marx did use the term *materialist* but only polemically in opposition to *idealism*. He was not concerned with the use of the term to indicate the belief that social phenomena can be reduced to the facts of the non-human environment. He did not, for example, believe that laws governing social phenomena could be reduced to psychological or biological laws, or that these sciences could be reduced to the physical sciences.

† Marx's Preface to Engels' *Karl Marx: A Contribution to the Critique of Political Economy* (1859).

It is this attitude and orientation that has made a contribution to the development of sociology, for it has led to a re-focusing of interest on social (including economic) relationships rather than upon social thought. Economic relationships define a person's class position, and it is classes, dynamically related in terms of the dialectical principle, that determine the course of human affairs, including men's thought, be it political, philosophical, religious, and so forth.* In the words of Joseph Schumpeter (1947), "we may say that it is our daily work which forms our minds, and that it is our location within the productive process which determines our outlook".

Now this influence of Marx on sociology is both general and specific. It is general in the sense that it helped to draw men's attention to the structure of relationships, and specific in that it helped to develop a branch of sociology known as the "sociology of knowledge", to which later writers such as Max Weber and, later still, Karl Mannheim (1936) have made notable contributions. This branch of the subject is interested in discerning the nature of the relationship between social thought and social structure, and most particularly social thought concerning politics; an able review of it is given by W. Stark (1958).

It must not be supposed that modern sociologists are primarily historicists. In fact, this is very far from being the case; but this tradition was undoubtedly one of the most formative influences on the subject which has grown partly as a result of its achievements and partly in reaction to it. We must turn now, however, to another intellectual tradition closely allied to historicism but which centres round the interest taken in the biological concept of evolution made popular by Charles Darwin and A. R. Wallace. The most outstanding figure here is Herbert Spencer (1820-1903).

---

* We think of Marx as a determinist, but we must remember that his historical determinism was emphasised as part of a polemic against Utopian Socialists who put their faith in reason. To Marx reason might show men their true situation but it did not help them to change it. He argued that whilst men behave in a rational manner, they do so only in terms of certain economic interests which are defined by the social situation in which men are rational. There are many rational acts in society, but the total consequences of them lead to the deterministic factor, for range of choice is limited by the situation in which men are placed. Thus, the employing classes must exploit the working classes, for if they failed to, they would be destroyed in the competitive process.

Spencer on Social Evolution and Social Types

Spencer tried to do for the social sciences what Darwin had done for the natural sciences, particularly biology, and biological analogies abound in his work. But we must not suppose that he was the originator of thought about social evolution, far from it; indeed, there is a very close link between the kind of argument put forward by Spencer and that, for instance, of Condorcet (1795). Consider this passage from the work of Condorcet:

"The first stage of civilisation observed amongst human beings is that of a small society whose members live by hunting and fishing, and know only how to make rather crude weapons and household utensils and to build or dig for themselves a place in which to live, but are already in possession of a language with which to communicate their needs, and a small number of moral ideas which serve as common laws of conduct; living families, conforming to general customs which take the place of laws, and even possessing a crude system of government."

And he goes on to describe this evolution of progress:

"Thus the progress of the human species was necessarily very slow; it could move forward only from time to time when it was favoured by exceptional circumstances. However, we see hunting, fishing, and the natural fruits of the earth replaced as a source of subsistence by food obtained from animals that man domesticates and that he learns to keep and breed. Later, a primitive form of agriculture developed; man was no longer satisfied with the fruits or plants that he came across by chance, but learnt to store them, to collect them around his dwelling, to sow or plant them, and to provide them with favourable conditions under which they could spread."

(Trans. 1955.)

Here we have a speculative attempt to describe the course of social evolution, and there were contemporaries of Spencer, too, also trying to fill in the details, to produce more elaborate accounts, and to solve some of the problems their labours posed. Such men as Lewis Morgan and Sir Edward Tylor were prominent figures in this tradition. Indeed, it is interesting to note that Morgan is

mentioned in a footnote on the first page of the Communist Manifesto (1885 edition), and the link between Marxist historicism and
evolutionary sociology is acknowledged at this point, even if the
relationship is an apparently covert one. Now, why do we select
Spencer for special mention? We do so because in his day and for
some time after his death he was very influential; he wrote a large
and popular book on sociology and he also attempted to make it
a coherent body of knowledge. Spencer was not only interested in
the evolutionary hypothesis, he was much taken by Comtean
method, and it may well be argued that much of his thought is a
reasonable development of Comte's.

How are we to describe what is meant by *social evolution*? Let
us take a fairly recent formulation drawn from Spencer's work by
the late A. R. Radcliffe-Brown (1952) which puts it in its briefest
form: "the development of life on earth constitutes a single process", namely, evolution. This is elaborated in the form of two
propositions:

1. "That both in the development of forms of organic life and
   in the development of forms of human social life there has
   been a process of diversification by which many different
   forms of organic life or of social life have been developed
   out of a very much smaller number of original forms.

2. "There has been a general trend of development by which
   more complex forms of structure and organisation (organic
   or social) have arisen from simpler forms." (p. 8.)

There does not seem to be very much difference of opinion
about this fundamental statement of the evolutionary hypothesis,
and doubtless most sociologists accept it with regard to social life
as biologists do with regard to organic life, but there is a good deal
of difference of opinion about the detailed ways in which social life
has evolved. Let us look at Spencer's work for a moment to see
what he had to say about it.

Apart from the quality of information at his disposal, which
was not always at all accurate, there is a general weakness about
his work, for we are obliged to recognise that Spencer presupposed
the truth of the evolutionary hypothesis rather than proved it.
Indeed, so willing was he to accept it that at one point in his work
he defined sociology as "the study of evolution in its most complex

form". His view of social evolution is outlined in a large two-volume work entitled *Principles of Sociology* (1876). The first volume brings together an immense amount of information that he collected largely as a result of a voluminous correspondence that he maintained with all kinds of people: travellers, explorers, journalists, missionaries, overseas administrators, and so forth. There are anthropological data of a physical, psychological, and social kind about primitive man, data about his ideas, beliefs, ritual practices, religious forms, and much else, and all this is cast in a framework of thought which aims to show how these various forms of social life have developed, and have developed according to the evolutionary hypothesis. Broadly speaking, his work is not dissimilar to that of others, but he goes on to argue that societies may be arranged in an order according to a few simple criteria, and this leads him to set out a morphology or classification of societies in a manner similar to the way a biologist classifies organic life. He discerned four types of societies: simple, compound, doubly compound, and trebly compound; each being divided and sub-divided.

A simple society is "one which forms a single working whole unsubjected to any other, and of which the parts co-operate, with or without a regulating centre, for certain public ends" (p. 539). Simple societies are divided according to the degree of centralised control; thus, there are headless simple societies, those with occasional headship, those with unstable headship, and those with stable headship. These are each in turn sub-divided accordingly as they are nomadic, semi-settled, or permanently settled. Overleaf is illustrated his scheme of classification of simple societies with some of the examples he gives of each kind.

A compound society is one where each social group has a chief under a supreme chief. There are by definition no headless societies, but apart from this omission the same sub-divisions are made. Doubly compound societies are completely settled and possess a variety of governments that have become subject to still higher government; there is also an elaborate ecclesiastical hierarchy. Here, he argues, custom has been crystallised into law, religion has become a complex phenomenon, there has been progress in the arts, and there is greater knowledge; moreover, towns have grown and roads linking them have been built. The trebly compound societies are the great civilised nations: ancient Mexico, Assyria, Egypt,

the Roman Empire, and the nineteenth-century European empires
of Britain, France, Germany, Italy, and Russia.

SIMPLE
SOCIETIES

Headless
- *Nomadic* (hunting) — Fuegians, some Australians, Bushmen.
- *Semi-settled*—most Esquimaux.
- *Settled* — Arafuras, Land Dyaks of Upper Sarawak River.

Occasional Headship
- *Nomadic* (hunting)—Tasmanians.
- *Semi-settled*—some Caribs.
- *Settled* — some Uaupés of the upper Rio Negro.

Vague and Unstable Headship
- *Nomadic* (hunting)—Andamanese, (pastoral)—some Bedouins.
- *Semi-settled*—some Esquimaux, Chinooks.
- *Settled*—Guiana tribes, Todas, Karens.

Stable Headship
- *Nomadic*—nil.
- *Semi-settled* — some Caribs, Patagonians.
- *Settled*—Pueblos.

In considering this social morphology we should perhaps remember Spencer's warning: "this classification must not be taken as
more than an approximation to the truth. In some cases data
furnished by travellers and others are inadequate; in some cases the
composition is so far transitional that it is difficult to say under
which of two heads it should come". The problem that faced him
was that of fitting data into preconceived pigeon-holes. We must
ask: for what purpose is this classification made? Spencer con-
cludes that there are societies of these different grades of composition, that societies of the same grade resemble one another, *and
that they develop in a similar order.* Finally, he says: "In this
order has social evolution gone on, and only in this order does it
appear to be possible". But it can surely be argued that the
introduction of the evolutionary hypothesis into the form of the
classification renders it scarcely surprising that he should conclude
with an evolutionary generalisation. Unilinear evolution has not
been demonstrated.

In a second morphology of societies, a simpler one, he makes "a classification based on unlikenesses between the kinds of activity which predominate, and on the resulting unlikenesses of organisation". He contrasts two types: the *militant* type and the *industrial* type. This is reminiscent of Comte's first and third stages of social development. A militant type of society is characterised by the place occupied by armed force; indeed, "the army is the nation mobilised while the nation is the quiescent army". Even in times of peace there is centralised control, a despotic and caste-like form of government with a military chief often as political head. There is also fairly tight ecclesiastical control, and not only are there normal means of political coercion, but there are supernatural punishments and religion supports the virtue of obedience; the ecclesiastical and the secular arms combine to maintain social order. There is in such a society what to-day we would call an ideology of the state; the individual is insignificant, the collectivity is all-important. Industry is rudimentary, and what there is is geared for war-like operations. The industrial type of society is described in terms of contrasts. It is a peaceful society with de-centralised control, and social life is maintained by agencies for the most part divorced from political control; indeed, there is little political power, and that is elective. Moreover, in religious matters there is private judgment, and there is, so to speak, an ideology of the freedom of the will of the individual. Free association obtains and there is a well developed privately-owned and privately-operated industry. But, again, Spencer notes that many variations of these two types exist, and these he attributes to racial mixtures, climatic and geographical differences, together with accidental historical factors. He puts forward this kind of argument:

> "Spain with its diverse peoples, Basque, Celtic, Gothic, Moorish, Jewish, partially mingled and partially localised, shows . . . that where races of strongly-contrasted natures have mixed . . . the equilibrium maintained so long as government keeps up coercive form, shows itself to be unstable when coercion relaxes." *

What Spencer is arguing is that the industrial type of society has evolved from the militant type. Social evolution is part of general

---

*It is interesting to compare this with Plato's remarks in *The Laws*, Book IV, 4, where there is a similar kind of observation.

evolution; the change is one from homogeneity to heterogeneity. The facts that are used to support this contention can be obtained, he claims, from empirical investigation. Again, however, we see weaknesses, for apart, for instance, from the unreasonableness of supposing that a militant type of society should be any less complex than an industrial one, he has introduced his evolutionary assumptions into his typology, thus leading him to seek examples supporting his contention whilst regarding those that do not as hybrids. There is a tendency throughout to imagine historical data where they are unknown. In other parts of his book we find Spencer, for instance, trying to argue that monogamous marriage is a late stage in the evolution of this general practice, and that originally men and women were sexually promiscuous. He is much more cautious than some other writers, such as L. H. Morgan (1877), and he does recognise that some evidence is unreliable, but many statements are made by him which are not only unsubstantiated but which are incapable of confirmation. As Radcliffe-Brown has pointed out, there has been a tendency to indulge in what he calls conjectural history. Where there are no written records, which by definition non-literate societies do not possess, historical explanations are likely to be fanciful. However, apart from this criticism, what evidence has been assembled from archaeology and ethnographic research during the present century has shown how vulnerable are such unilinear evolutionary schemes.

There is, however, an interesting feature of this later classification of Spencer's, for whilst it does little to assist in his main aim it points to a covert shift in his interest. It is indeed a forerunner of other typologies and shows how sociologists began to ask: How far and in what ways does modern industrial society differ from the simple, non-literate, small, closely-knit society? The emphasis is rather more on structure than history, description of significant aspects of modern society rather than speculations as to how modern society came to be what it is. This slight shift that we see in Spencer heralds the change from sociology as a philosophical and historical discipline to sociology as a descriptive and systematic discipline. This will become clearer as we proceed.

There is one other element in Spencer's thought that must be mentioned before passing on, and this concerns his attempt to discuss social life in terms of a biological analogy. Thus he tried to argue that societies are organisms. Just as a biological organism has a structure, so has society, and just as with increasing size organisms become more complex so also do societies. The analogy is drawn at length: the primitive society is like a simple organism, the complex society, when examined in detail, can be seen to be made up of parts similar to the parts of a complex organism. There are certain needs shared by both, and they both have the means to meet these needs. Here is an example of his account:

> "With increased pressure of traffic has come, in addition to the road, the railway; which in place of a single channel for movement in both directions, habitually has a double channel —up-line and down-line—analogous to the double set of tubes through which, in a superior animal, blood proceeds from the centre and towards the centre." (I, p. 497.)

Or again, in likening government to the neuro-muscular apparatus, he proceeds with unconscious irony:

> "Strange as the assertion will be thought, our Houses of Parliament discharge in the social economy functions which are, in sundry respects, comparable to those discharged by the cerebral masses in a vertebrate animal."

There are many weaknesses in this analogical endeavour, but we need not dwell on them unduly. Suffice it to say that the analogy is too broad and general to be useful; it fails to demonstrate the particular ways in which the ends served are related to each other; his use of the terms *higher* and *lower* is not clear, for a higher entity in his scheme of things should have a centralised control and unified action. But this leads him into inconsistencies, as where he places the militant type of society in inferior position to an industrial one; and, of course, there are many places where the parallel breaks down. Is there, then, no value in this? Considering the history of sociology it may be argued that Spencer did succeed in focusing attention on the structure of society and, moreover, on social functions. We shall have to leave till later a discussion of these important concepts, but we may note that his was one of the more important attempts to analyse societies and compare them in terms of their parts and the manner in which the parts serve the whole, enabling it to continue as an on-going concern. Indeed, it was this extensive use of the comparative method that has rendered him such

an important formative influence in sociology, particularly in this
country.

Hobhouse on Social and Moral Evolution

One distinguished sociologist to be influenced by Spencer was
L. T. Hobhouse (1864-1929), who by extensive application of the
comparative method did much to advance the study of social institutions, whilst at the same time rendering a more sophisticated
account of social evolution, or, as he called it, social development
(1924). Taking an encyclopaedic view of the subject he tried to
relate his study of social change to his ethical philosophy. To do
this he deduced from his conception of development four criteria:
scale of organisation in society, degree of efficiency in control over
natural resources and direction of activities, degree of co-operation
of people to their mutual advantage, and freedom of scope for
personal development. In the words of his biographer, Morris
Ginsberg, Hobhouse "argues that in accordance with his ethical
theory, complete development, that is advance in all four directions,
involves the most ample and consistent fulfilment of human purposes and is therefore a rational end, or good, while partial or
one-sided developments may be good or bad according as they affect
the whole" (1947).

It is not altogether clear that his criteria for social development
are as ethically neutral as he claimed, but in the process of carrying out his impressive plan he advanced the use of the comparative
method and also gave strength to the idea that societies may be
regarded as systems of interdependent parts, where the parts adapt
themselves in such a manner that the whole system is maintained
as a process. An instance of the use of the comparative method is
to be seen in the detailed statistical study carried out by him in
collaboration with Wheeler and Ginsberg (1915); a similar, later
pursuit in the U.S.A. has led to the development of the Yale Cross-
Cultural Survey under the direction of G. P. Murdock (1940).

Historicism Criticised

As historicism, particularly as seen in Comte and Marx, has
been a powerful factor in the history of sociology, and as the unilinear evolutionary sociology of Spencer is not unrelated to this
tradition, let us pause before continuing to note that in recent years

the entire body of assumptions of historicism has been trenchantly criticised, particularly in Britain by W. H. Walsh (1951) and K. R. Popper (1944-5 and 1957).

Whilst it is too large a task to examine in detail these criticisms, we shall briefly point to one or two of the more important of them. Thus Popper believes that the entire attempt to predict the future is mistaken. His argument is that the course of human history is strongly influenced by the growth of human knowledge, including scientific knowledge, and that we cannot predict by rational or scientific methods the future growth of our scientific knowledge, and consequently we cannot predict the future course of history. But more specifically he has examined what he calls the pro-naturalistic type of historicism, having in mind principally Comte and those influenced by him, and he asks: Is there a law of evolution? He maintains that the search for such a law cannot fall within the scope of scientific method, either in biology or in sociology. "The evolution of life on earth, or of human society, is a unique historical process. Such a process we may assume proceeds in accordance with all kinds of causal laws, for example, the laws of mechanics, of chemistry, of heredity and segregation, of natural selection, etc. Its description, however, is not a law, but only a singular historical statement. Universal laws make assertions concerning some unvarying order . . . we cannot hope to test a universal hypothesis nor to find a natural law acceptable to science if we are for ever confined to the observation of one unique process" (1957, pp. 108-9). Nor is it very profitable, he goes on to say, to speak of evolutionary trends, for there is a danger in following Comte in this that we confuse a trend with a law. They are quite different. A trend is always reversible and forms no sound basis for prediction of the future. The poverty of historicism generally lies in the inability to imagine a change in the conditions of change, and this *par excellence* is the criticism that must be levelled, for instance, at the work of Marx.

It is perhaps worth while to pause at this point in order to suggest that much of this early tradition in sociology, particularly associated with the work of Comte, Marx, and Spencer on the one hand, but also that of the reformers and social surveyors in Britain, to whom we shall refer later, on the other hand, was the outcome, and in so far as it still persists is directed by a suspension, of the

belief that human destinies, both individual and corporate, are controlled by a God whose will it is impossible and impious to question.
After all, the natural scientists in the course of their work had
experienced many difficulties because of the scruples of the religious
people of their day, and the same was no less true of those who
turned their minds to social phenomena. Yet despite the decline in
religious belief there seems to have been a reluctance to believe that
humanity was subject to the whim of any wind that blows, that man
is subject to capricious forces. Indeed, this reluctance, combined with the growing prestige of the natural sciences, appears
largely to be responsible for the willingness of thinkers to search
for laws, and, in particular, laws that would assure them of man's
destiny; laws of progress, in fact.

If men could be assured of human progress it was natural that
they should seek to understand the conditions under which it
obtained, and this with the object of engineering it. There are
clearly features of Marx's work that demonstrate this, and whilst
it is doubtful if Marx had any very direct influence on the reformers
and early social scientists in Britain, the scientific tradition of observation of facts most certainly did. Thus developed the tradition of
social investigation with practical ends in view, for it was clear that
in Britain social progress was being impeded by social conditions.
Much good came of this tradition, as we shall see, but there were
some unfortunate consequences. One of these was the identification of the social scientist, or sociologist, with the "good citizen",
and following from this an undue influence on problem-selection
in social research of practical problems rather than intellectual ones.
The two are, of course, not unconnected, but too much emphasis
on social problems inhibits the development of an intellectual
discipline. The relationship between theory and observation is an
intricate one, but that there must be a relationship has been demonstrated time and again in sociological research.

Durkheim on Social Order and Sociological Method

We turn now to a group of writers who mark the beginning of
quite a radical reorientation of sociology. The most notable of
these, perhaps, is the French sociologist, Émile Durkheim (1858-
1917), and in many ways he is the most interesting because initially
he stood squarely in the Comtean positivist tradition, which was,

of course, shared by Spencer. Yet in his early work (1893) we find him being critical of Spencer's view of the nature of social order, not, be it noted, of his evolutionary view of social change, for Durkheim has little to say about this. This distinction between social order and social change is seen in Comte's division of sociology into social statics and social dynamics; the former seeks the laws of inter-connection of the parts, the latter the laws of change of the whole through time.* Now, Spencer held the view that social order or stability results from the mutual advantages that are derived from social intercourse, and that the higher type of society, the industrial type, depends for stability on contractual relationships. Durkheim rightly pointed out that this is unsound, for contractual relationships are entered into in terms of a body of tacit but binding rules which are not part of contractual agreements. Such rules, for instance, determine what are and what are not valid contracts, as, for example, when a contractual agreement is rendered void through being secured by force. Again, he notes that sometimes a contracting party is required to accept obligations which were not part of the original contract.

This general problem of how social order obtains is one which Durkheim pursued in his later works, and in so doing contributed both directly and indirectly to the theoretical development of sociology, departing indeed from both the positivist and utilitarian traditions in which sociology had developed, as Talcott Parsons has very ably described (1937).

In his early work, too, Durkheim is important for the quite explicit distinction he made between sociology and other social disciplines, and in particular for distinguishing it from psychology. This is largely the burden of his famous small book on method (1895), but it is illustrated in his monograph on suicide (1897). In his discussion of method he said that sociologists should study *social facts* and that they should study them as things (*comme les choses*).

What Durkheim meant was that the sociologist should study the facts of social life as distinct from, say, biological or psychological

---

* The use of the terms "statics" and "dynamics" in sociology is misleading, for these terms have been borrowed from the physical sciences, and as K. R. Popper says: "the kind of society which the sociologist calls 'static' is precisely analogous to such physical systems as the physicist would call 'dynamic'" (1957, p. 112).

processes, but such facts should be ones which are general throughout the extent of a given society, and, he added, "at a given stage
in the evolution of that society". In this he distinguishes a social
fact from a psychological fact, the latter being general to humanity
—like volition or cognition. It is necessary, perhaps, to point out
that when he said it should be general throughout a society he
did not mean that a fact was something common to all members.
Crime represents a social fact, but not all men in a given society
are criminal; yet it is to be found with varying incidence in all
societies, and, he argued, it has a certain incidence in a society of
a given type. Moreover, such social facts as Durkheim had in mind
exercise constraint on the members of society; they are, to use his
terms, "exterior" and "resistant"; they are objective and they influence people's behaviour to the extent, in this example, that crime
leads to measures to deal with it.

In his study of suicide Durkheim does much more than tell us
something interesting about this social phenomenon. He begins by
examining a variety of types of explanation of suicide. Thus any
particular suicide may be explicable in terms of the pyschological
effects of mental illness, emotional disturbance from domestic infeli-
city or financial loss, and so forth. In all these cases, explanation is
cast in terms of motivation and, as such, is psychological. But he goes
on to demonstrate that when all the suicides that occur in a society
in any one period are so classified and compared with the numbers
occurring at another period, whilst the proportions falling into each
class tend to remain constant, the general rate of suicide may be
different, and that the rates may indeed show wide variations. It
is this last phenomenon that Durkheim designates as a social fact
requiring investigation, and it must be studied, he argues, at its
own specific level, for it is inappropriate to explain it in psychological terms of motivation.

Now, if an explanation in terms of motives is impossible, it
follows that there is something conditioning the suicide rate over
which individuals have no control. We should look, he says, for
a social factor instead of a psychological one, and he found this in
the kind of attachment an individual has to his social group.

In presenting his argument Durkheim analysed several types of
suicide. Thus, one type he calls *altruistic*, and by this term denotes
the case where the individual has a very close tie to his social group,

so much so that his own individual existence is of small account compared with the social obligations that are laid on him. The elderly person in a nomadic tribe who is too infirm to keep up with the group ends his own life in the interests of the group, or another example is the Hindu practice of *suttee*, where a widow throws herself on her husband's funeral pyre. Durkheim found statistical comparisons of suicide rates among soldiers and civilians to be instructive, for the rate is higher among military personnel, and it is higher among officers than other ranks, and higher among those with long service than among recruits, which indicates the irrelevance of poverty or hardship. In fact, there is no correlation between poverty and suicide generally. Here Durkheim points to the fact that among military men, and particularly those of long standing, there is a high value placed upon the social group of which a man is a member and a relative carelessness about the individual's own life. We are familiar with the phenomenon in the case of the Japanese officer and soldier or the Prussian officer, each of whom is strongly attached to his military code of honour.

There is, however, a different kind of suicide, namely *egoistic* suicide, where the individual is without firm group attachments. Thus a statistical comparison shows that, generally speaking, married people have a lower suicide rate than single, widowed, or divorced people, and that among married people it is lower in the case of couples with children than for those without them. Again, he compared the rates for Catholics with those for Protestants and found them higher among the latter. Here he argues that the Catholic is more strongly attached to his Church than the Protestant. His empirical facts are not seriously in dispute, but his argument is not altogether sound, for although both Churches strongly forbid suicide, Durkheim failed to see that there is not so much a differential group-attachment as a difference in the content of the relationship the religious individual has to his group. As Parsons points out, a Protestant of good standing must assume responsibility and exercise freedom of decision relatively more than a Catholic, and he goes on: "By placing the Protestant in a particular relation to his religious group, by placing a particularly heavy load of religious responsibility upon him, strains are created of which, in a relatively high proportion of cases, the result is suicide" (1937, p. 333).

This emendation of the Durkheimian analysis is of special interest, for it focuses attention on the nature of the body of values which govern behaviour; such values are external to the individual and may in the case of altruistic suicide directly enjoin this specific act, or they may be of such a nature as to create strains and stresses so that indirectly they influence the suicide rate.

Durkheim, in fact, discerned yet another kind of suicide, which he called *anomic*, and this has some bearing on the previous illustration, but he only saw this in relation to the fact that there are statistical correlations between periods of marked economic depression, when the rate is high, and periods of marked economic prosperity, when the rate, surprisingly, is also high. The two sets of facts, he says, must surely be due to the same set of circumstances underlying the diversity of instances. He argues that the scheme of values in a society, whilst operating differently at different levels of society, conditions people's expectations, and that periods of acute economic depression equally with periods of sudden prosperity tend to disturb these expectations, resulting in confusion, loss of orientation, and so increasing the strains and stresses which in a proportion of cases lead to suicides.

What is important in this empirical study is that, on the one hand, it has shown that there is a level of sociological analysis different from the level on which psychological discussion of individual behaviour takes place, whilst, on the other hand, it has pointed out the importance of studying values, and most particularly the common values of a society. Of course, sociological explanations should be congruent with psychological ones, and in the case of studies of suicide this necessity prompted the work of Durkheim's pupil, M. Halbwachs (1930), and more recently it has been fundamental to the study by Henry and Short (1954). For the purposes of this brief history of sociology we have said enough about Durkheim's work, save to note in concluding that it was the rules and customs that reflect the values of a society which he thought should be the proper subject of the sociologist's investigation; in other words, the comparative study of social institutions.

German Sociology—Simmel and Weber

In Germany at the beginning of this century two main traditions in sociology had developed, and neither was much influenced by the positivist sociology of Comte and Spencer. These two traditions may be said to be the forerunners of the modern tendency for sociology to bifurcate into what may be called macro- and micro-sociology. The first tradition is an historical-sociological one and the second a rather narrower, more analytical one concerned with types of social groupings and types of relationships found in them. The former developed against a background of philosophical ideal-ism, but has been much influenced by Marx; it may in some ways be said to be an attempt to come to terms with the Marxist thesis, and it is much concerned with the study of modern urban, indus-trial society and its development. Two writers only will be men-tioned by way of illustration: Max Weber (1864-1920) and Georg Simmel (1858-1918).

Simmel's writings are various and not very systematic, but he considered analytically a number of related topics, such as the nature of reciprocal relationships, the kinds of relationships that obtain in small groups, comparing two-member groups with three-member groups. He examined forms of relationship such as authority and subordination. He investigated and compared differ-ent forms of conflict, and he wrote a celebrated essay on the large metropolitan city and its effects on personality (*trans.* 1950).

Many of these lines of thought have in recent years been taken up, often independently of Simmel's work, and among those who have contributed to this modern micro-sociological development, often called *group dynamics*,* we may mention G. Homans (1951), R. F. Bales (1951), L. Festinger (1954), and J. Klein (1956). We shall have occasion to refer to some of the more recent work falling into this category later, particularly when considering kinship, family, and neighbourly relations in Part III.

Max Weber's work is much more ambitious in scope and inten-tion, and may be said to be an attempt to answer the question: How did capitalism as a unique method of organising resources come to be developed in Europe and America? To do this he contributed to sociology two distinct ideas; one was the concept of the *ideal type* and the other was a unified notion of causality and under-standing.

An ideal type is neither what we think ought to be, nor is it necessarily what others have thought ought to be, but is a collection

* The term "dynamics" is correctly used in describing this work.

of features of an entity that are logically consistent and which render its existence possible. For example, one of his most important concepts was the ideal type he called *bureaucracy* (*trans.* 1948). This, in short, may be described in terms of certain properties, such as an hierarchical organisation of appointed employees chosen in terms of their suitability to perform administrative tasks; these tasks to be carried out according to a body of formal rules, and part of the task to be the recording of administrative acts for future reference; each official to have a specified and recognised sphere of competence, to be prevented from appropriating his post, and to be prevented from mixing his domestic affairs with those he is concerned with as an official. Quite clearly these are features of various modern organisations, but especially of the civil service.

This example is one of a general ideal type, but Weber used it in his profound analysis of another phenomenon in which he was mainly interested, namely the historical ideal type of *capitalism* (*trans.* 1947). His discussion of this, together with his attempt to discern the principal factors giving rise to it, and most particularly his endeavour to relate types of socio-economic structure to systems of religious beliefs, constitute some of the imposing achievements of historical sociology, and has given a considerable lead to latter-day studies of modern industrial society, as, for example, in the work of J. Schumpeter (1947); but also his work has influenced others carrying out studies of the ancient world, a recent example being the monumental study of "hydraulic" societies by K. Wittfogel (1957).

Although Weber stressed the importance of rigorously defined concepts used with all the resources of scientific method, he also held that something more than correlations was required in the social sciences, and in an endeavour to provide explanations involving both causality and meaning he introduced the notion, which owes much to the work of Dilthey (Hodges, 1952), of understanding (*verstehen*). He tried to do this in terms of types of social action where action is seen to be related to motives, but he stressed the point that the subjective meaning of behaviour of a person or group must be accessible; it must be related to our common knowledge of humanity.

Weber's contribution to methodology was such that whilst recognising that sociology is to be distinguished from history and psychology he did much to relate them. This task of relating the sciences, particularly sociology and psychology, is one which Parsons and others are endeavouring to accomplish in our own time (1951).

American Sociology Between the Wars

Sociological research developed rapidly after the First World War, and even more so during and after the Second, especially in America, but also in Britain and France; since the last war there has been also a resurgence in Germany. We can but very briefly indicate the general lines along which this work has been carried out. In America a reaction to the encyclopaedic and evolutionary writings of the early sociologists like L. H. Morgan, Lester Ward, W. G. Sumner, and F. H. Giddings led to studies that could be described as raw empiricism. Eschewing theoretical constructions, sociologists took to making detailed unsystematic observations of social life in America, both urban and rural, but with a gradually greater emphasis on the large city.

The rapidly expanding cosmopolitan nature of America's industrial cities after the First World War with large immigrant populations was a fruitful field for sociological studies. As E. A. Shils says of the nineteen-twenties, they were "characterised by a vivid, energetic curiosity about the rich and mysterious texture of metropolitan life" (1947). Some of the works he had in mind included a notable series of monographs written by students of Robert Park, among them being F. Thrasher's *The Gang*, L. Wirth's *The Ghetto*, Zorbaugh's *The Gold Coast and the Slum*, Nels Anderson's *The Hobo*, and Reckless's *Taxi Dance Hall*. Another outstanding work was *The Polish Peasant in Europe and America* (1920) by W. I. Thomas and F. Znaniecki, and there were other studies of ethnic groups, particularly of the American Negro.

An influential development in anthropology, stimulated largely by Ruth Benedict (1934), which gave rise to the study of cultures as wholes, and by Ralph Linton (1936), which placed emphasis on role-playing, in turn affected sociological studies of urban life, as may be seen in the work of R. and H. Lynd (1929 and 1937). Statistical techniques, allied to a general anthropological outlook, may be seen in the work of Lloyd Warner in studying Newburyport and which resulted in the several volumes of the Yankee City Series.

British Social Science

The development of sociology in Britain may be said to have followed two quite distinct lines. On the one hand there were the more speculative kinds of writers like the early moral philosophers such as Adam Ferguson and John Millar in Scotland, and evolutionists like Spencer and Hobhouse in England, but on the other hand there was also the social science tradition, largely influenced by philanthropists and reformers. Thus whilst we may note the tradition of reform in which the names of John Howard, Edwin Chadwick, and Florence Nightingale feature we should also note the many able and energetic people who sponsored and maintained the National Association for the Promotion of Social Science, founded by Lord Brougham and others in 1857 and which held annual conferences in the major cities of the kingdom until the 1880s. This was a tradition of data collection designed to compile evidence which would influence legislators and administrators. The National Association was merely one of a number of reforming societies, some of which had been established early in the century like the Society for Bettering the Condition and Increasing the Comforts of the Poor, but it was an association which deliberately tried to bring precision and method into its work; it was interested in *social science*. This combination of reforming zeal and meticulous attention to facts has left its mark on social studies in Britain as may be seen for example in the work of Charles Booth (1891) and Benjamin Seebohm Rowntree (1901), both of them philanthropists who carried out surveys into the nature and incidence of poverty, and if it has to be said that they did little for the development of sociological theory they made valuable contributions in the development of techniques of research and, of course, they were of political importance in informing and marshalling public opinion. This kind of social survey enquiry has proliferated greatly in recent years as social surveys of all kinds have been carried out into problems not only of poverty, but of housing and old age, investigations into the nature of social needs and the extent to which both statutory and voluntary social services are meeting or failing to meet them, and also polling of various kinds related either to political opinions or to market demands.

Yet whilst there has been a development of empirical research techniques there has also been a continuation of the more theoretical and speculative tradition which, as we indicated at the beginning of the chapter, sprang from the eighteenth century French writers and the thought of Auguste Comte. This was a strong tradition in Scotland in the late eighteenth century, a tradition, indeed, closely related to moral philosophy. Montesquieu's *De L'Esprit des Lois* (1748), one of the first sociological works of the Enlightenment, greatly influenced Adam Ferguson's essay on the *History of Civil Society* (1767); John Millar also helped to form sociological thought, an early and influential essay of his appearing in a revised form in 1779 as *The Origin of the Distinction of Ranks*. Millar and Ferguson are two only of the prominent figures of the time. Similarly, the work of Herbert Spencer and Sir Henry Maine in England led to a development in sociology, partly to be seen in the growth of social anthropology, partly in moral philosophy and the study of legal institutions and which contributed to comparative studies of social institutions and to the establishment of sociology in the University of London, where the first chair was founded in 1906 and occupied by L. T. Hobhouse, whose work we referred to earlier. The growth of social anthropology in Britain, like the development of cultural anthropology in America, has had its effect on the history of sociology, for it emphasised the importance of comparative studies, the examination of the customs and beliefs of various peoples, and above all the over-riding importance of not only making careful observations of human behaviour but also of thinking about it in an effective way. It was largely in the work of Bronislaw Malinowski and A. R. Radcliffe-Brown at the Universities of London and Oxford respectively that this came about. Thus Radcliffe-Brown's emphasis on the concept of *structure* and his notion that societies may be studied as natural *systems* led to a diminished regard for what he called conjectural history and the adoption of the practice of trying to discern the similarities of structural principles underlying diverse social practices by the thorough-going use of the comparative method. The general tenor of much of this book is the result of the contribution he made to our ways of thinking about human society. But Radcliffe-Brown and Malinowski also taught in the U.S.A. and made their mark there on American anthropological studies. Their influence, together with that of Max Weber, gave a new turn to sociological study in America, especially just before and after World War II, and we will close this chapter which attempts to outline the growth of the subject by a brief reference to these more theoretical developments.

Systematic Sociology

Perhaps the reaction to American empiricism may be best seen in the work of Talcott Parsons, although it should not be forgotten that the encyclopaedic tradition of the subject which we associate with European scholars was represented for many years in the work of W. G. Sumner and F. H. Giddings and more recently at Harvard University by Pitirim Sorokin. Parsons himself had studied in German and British Universities and was largely responsible for rendering the works of Durkheim, Weber, and Pareto familiar to American sociologists. His later work, however, stresses the notion of the social system, which he sees as one among several; the others being personality and cultural systems. It is his intention to show the points of articulation between these systems, and by the elaboration of abstract conceptual schemes to indicate the nature of sociological theory and its relevance to modern social investigation.

Another American writer to advance the development of theory is Robert K. Merton, whose famous essay on "Manifest and Latent Functions" is a major contribution to the kind of approach to the subject this book makes, for Merton is keen to point to both the intended consequences of human actions and their unintended consequences. The assumption behind his discussion is again that societies are systems, that they may be regarded as differentiated wholes whose parts are related, as we say, systematically. Most modern sociology accepts this basic assumption, but of course there are differences both in the style and manner of writing on sociological theory among sociologists, so that we see different emphases placed on the extent to which human society is an integrated whole, and then again we find sociologists having different ideas as to the constitution of a social system, some regarding it as a set of social institutions, others as made up of groups or groupings, and yet others who emphasise organisations as the essential units of the total system. In the next chapter we shall spell out some of the elements of sociological theory, showing how it helps the sociologist to orient himself to his subject and how it provides him with the intellectual tools of his trade. A warning, however, is not out of place at this point, for it has to be remembered that theory is to be judged pragmatically; it is either helpful or it is not, and when it ceases to be helpful it must be revised. Indeed, sociological theory is always a subject for critical appraisal in the light of empirical sociological studies and their results. The kind of approach outlined in this short introduction to sociology has already been the subject of criticism, and it is entirely reasonable that it should be. We may look forward to modifications of the views that societies may usefully be regarded as social systems, but this approach, as will be seen, has in the past been fruitful (and indeed has played a very big part in the history of the subject), and it may for this reason be commended to the novice.

BIBLIOGRAPHY AND FURTHER READING

Bales, R. F., *Interaction Process Analysis*, 1951 (Addison-Wesley).
Benedict, Ruth, *Patterns of Culture*, 1934 (Routledge and Kegan Paul).
Booth, Charles, *Survey of London Life and Labour*, 1891, 1904, 17 vols.
Radcliffe-Brown, A. R., *Structure and Function in Primitive Society*, 1951 (Cohen and West).
Cohen, P. S., *Modern Social Theory*, 1968, (Heinemann).
Comte, Auguste, *Positive Philosophy*, trans. H. Martineau, 1895.
de Condorcet, A. N., *Sketch for a historical picture of the progress of the human mind*, 1795, trans. 1955 by J. Barraclough (Weidenfeld and Nicolson).
Durkheim, E., *Division of Labour in Society*, 1893, trans. 1947 (Free Press).
Rules of Sociological Method, 1895, trans. 1938 (Free Press).
Suicide, 1897, trans. 1951 (Free Press), 1952 (Routledge and Kegan Paul).
Festinger, L., "A Theory of Social Comparison Processes", *Human Relations*, VII, 1954.
Ginsberg, M., *Reason and Unreason in Society*, 1947 (Longmans).
Halbwachs, M., *Les Causes du Suicide*, 1930 (Librairie Félix Alcan).
Henderson, L. J., *Pareto's General Sociology*, 1935 (Harvard).
Henry, A. F., and Short, J. F., *Suicide and Homicide*, 1954 (Free Press).

Hodges, H. A., *The Philosophy of Wilhelm Dilthey*, 1952 (Routledge and Kegan Paul).

Hobhouse, L. T., *Social Development*, 1924 (Allen and Unwin).

Hobhouse, L. T., Wheeler, and Ginsberg, *The Material Culture and Social Institutions of the Simpler Peoples*, 1915 (Chatto and Windus).

Homans, G. C., *The Human Group*, 1951 (Routledge and Kegan Paul).

Klein, J., *The Study of Groups*, 1956 (Routledge and Kegan Paul).

Linton, R., *The Study of Man*, 1936 (Appleton-Century).

Lynd, R. and H., *Middletown*, 1929 (Harcourt Brace).
Middletown in Transition, 1937 (Harcourt Brace).

Mannheim, K., *Ideology and Utopia*, trans. 1936 (Routledge and Kegan Paul).

Merton, R. K., *Social Theory and Social Structure*, 1949, Rev. Ed. 1957 (Free Press), also *On Theoretical Sociology*, 1967 (Free Press Paperback).

Mitchell, G. D., *A Hundred Years of Sociology*, 1968 (Duckworth) and (Edit.) *A Dictionary of Sociology*, 1968 (Routledge and Kegan Paul).

Morgan, L. H., *Ancient Society*, 1877.

Murdock, G. P., "The Cross-Cultural Survey", Amer. Soc. Rev., 1940.

Parsons, Talcott, *The Structure of Social Action*, 1937 (Free Press). *Essays in Sociological Theory: Pure and Applied*, 1949, Rev. Ed. 1954 (Free Press).

Parsons, Talcott, *The Social System*, 1952 (Tavistock).

Parsons, Talcott, and Shils, E. A., *Towards a General Theory of Action*, 1951 (Harvard).

Popper, K. R., "The Poverty of Historicism", *Economica*, 1944-5. *The Poverty of Historicism*, 1957 (Routledge and Kegan Paul).

Rowntree, B. S., *Poverty, a study of town life*, 1901 (Macmillan).

Schumpeter, J., *Capitalism, Socialism and Democracy*, 1947 (Allen and Unwin).

Shils, E. A., "The Present Situation in American Sociology", *Pilot Papers*, II. 2, 1947.

Simey, T. S. and M. B., *Charles Booth: Social Scientist*, 1960 (O.U.P.).

Simmel, G., *The Sociology of Georg Simmel*, Ed. K. Wolff, 1950 (Free Press).
Sorokin, Pitirim A., *Society, Culture and Personality*, 1947 (Harper).
Spencer, H., *Principles of Sociology*, 1876.
Stark, W., *The Sociology of Knowledge*, 1958 (Routledge and Kegan Paul).
Thomas, W. I., and Znaniecki, F., *The Polish Peasant in Europe and America*, 1920.
Walsh, W. H., *An Introduction to Philosophy of History*, 1951 (Hutchinson's Univ. Lib.).
Weber, M., *The Theory of Social and Economic Organisation*, 1947 (trans. from Wirtschaft u. Gesellschaft, Vol. I (Wm. Hodge and Co.)
    From Max Weber: Essays in Sociology, H. Gerth and C. W. Mills (Eds.), 1948 (Routledge and Kegan Paul).
Wittfogel, K., *Oriental Despotism*, 1957 (Yale).

CHAPTER II

SOCIETIES REGARDED AS SOCIAL SYSTEMS

Definitions, Distinctions, and Descriptive Terms

When in common parlance we speak of a *society* we usually have in mind a collection of people who have this in common— that they belong in some sense to one another. Often we are apt to regard them as occupying and sharing a certain defined territory, but a moment's reflection will show that this is neither a necessary nor a sufficient condition; witness, for example, the Isma'ilis, who constitute a Moslem sect scattered over many parts of the world but who are united under the Aga Khan. We may, instead, point to a certain body of knowledge shared by people about their past or about their present relationships with others. Or we may think of a people who regard themselves as being different in certain ways from others. The fact is that the term *society* is loosely used; indeed it is difficult to be precise in using it because it is such a commonly-used word, but intuitively it conveys some meaning, and to this extent it is useful provided we do not lay too great an intellectual weight upon it. Usually we speak of the British as being a society, or we may refer to the BaMangwato of Bechuanaland in Africa, or the Pueblo Indians of America, or the Gipsies as each being a society.

One thing we can be clear about; we are thinking of more than a mere *aggregate* when we talk about a society. All blue-eyed people constitute a statistical aggregate but not a society, although if they came together in some organised form to further their inter- ests as, say, against brown-eyed people, we would be inclined to regard them as a society or, at least, a *social group*. The difference between a statistical group or aggregate on the one hand and a social group or society on the other is the difference between a mere collection of units and a collection where the units are related in terms of interaction; here, of course, the units are persons.

Social life, like all life, is a process. Some sociologists prefer to say that they are studying aspects of this process, but for many others the concrete and observable reality is society. There have been many attempts to define it. To give one example, that of S. F. Nadel: "By society we can only mean an aggregate of human beings bound together in some unity, that is, acting in an integrated and regular manner, and possessed of some degree of permanence and stability" (1953). Yet these terms "integrated", "regulated", "permanence", and "stability" are not very precise terms, and indeed could each be used to help define each other. The word "society" is not, in fact, precisely used at all, but perhaps this does not matter very much; it is much more important to use in a precise manner other descriptive and analytic terms, and it is the purpose of this chapter to say something about these.

It is clear that the sociologist is concerned with collections of people who share certain kinds of knowledge. And this knowledge is that which a person has about other people's behaviour. He knows what to expect of others and what other people expect of him. Now such knowledge of behaviour is possible because a very great deal of human behaviour is standardised and regular. If we enter a shop we have a fairly clear idea of what kind of human behaviour to expect when we face the shop assistant. To be sure, there may be variations in details, but, broadly speaking, we expect him to find out what we want to purchase just as he will expect that we have it in mind to make a purchase. Behaviour here is fairly rigidly defined, even to the form of words used in the exchange of information. And in most situations the forms of behaviour appropriate to the situation are fairly clearly defined. The process of growing up is largely one in which the child learns these things, and learns them by a process of trial and error so that when judgment errs the situation is redefined more correctly. What is learned is the body of *norms* governing social behaviour. There are, of course, many cues indicating what norms are appropriate for the various situations in which people interact; a common one is the use of uniforms or insignia to tell us, for example, that this man is a bus conductor or that woman a receptionist, and so identified we act towards them in terms of a body of mutually-held norms.

Social Positions and Social Roles

Now the sociologist finds it necessary to go beyond the use of descriptive terms like bus conductor, receptionist, shop assistant, customer, and, therefore, he formulates analytic terms. If we

consider, say, the shop assistant and the customer, we say that they
are persons occupying, respectively, the *social positions* of assistant
and customer, and we go on to describe their behaviour as such
as *role-playing*. In much the same way as an actor on the stage
plays a part or *role*, the assistant plays one role and the customer
another but complementary role. Roles, then, are related to positions, and just as with the actor's role these roles may be played
well or badly according to the norms that are held to govern
behaviour connected with these positions. Hence we may hear
people speak of a good or helpful assistant or a willing or difficult
customer. *Social position** and *role* are analytic terms; they have
a more general quality than do the concrete descriptive terms to
which they have reference.

An important distinction may be made between *ascribed* and
achieved social positions. That is to say, a distinction between
social positions which are given a person, over which he has no
control initially, and those which can be striven for. Thus the
position of a boy in a family is ascribed in terms both of sex
and juniority, whilst the place of the child in his school class is
achieved, and so also is his occupation likely to be when he grows
up. Societies vary considerably in the relative distribution of
ascribed and achieved positions; the former carrying greater weight
in a simple society than in a modern industrial society, where there
is greater emphasis on achievement and particularly of occupational positions.

Clearly there is an advantage in being able to relate in our
discussion a wide range of social phenomena, and to do so by the
use of a few terms. It will be readily appreciated that a person
occupies many positions and plays many roles. A person may
be a father, a brother, an elder son, and an uncle, and these roles
are both complex and different in each case. The playing of them
depends on a variety of circumstances, for one is a father in relation
to one's children and an uncle in relation to nephews and nieces,
and so forth. Moreover, such a person will occupy other positions :
he may be a clerk, a motorist, a member of a tennis club, a churchman, a voter, etc.

* The term "social position" is here preferred to that of "status", which is
often used, in order to avoid ambiguities in the meaning given the latter term.
Cf. Davis (1948), Chapter 4.

Sometimes the sociologist is concerned with the effects on role-playing of a person occupying several social positions. To what extent and in what ways, he asks, does a man's position as a churchman affect his role in the position of a voter? Does the one role have a bearing on the playing of another role? Here discussion centres round what are known as *multiple roles*.

Yet another kind of enquiry, outlined by Merton (1957), is connected with the concept of *role-set*. From what has been said it might be assumed that there is one fairly clearly defined role appropriate to each social position, but the facts of social reality are much more complex. There are, indeed, frequently many roles related to any one social position. For any social position there is what Merton calls "a complement of role-relationships in which persons are involved", and he illustrates this with reference to the school teacher who by virtue of his position has roles to play *vis à vis* his pupils, his colleagues, his head-teacher, parents, members of the school board, his professional association, and so forth. There is room for a considerable degree of conflict in such a role-set, for what the parent feels should constitute the education of his child is not necessarily what the school board considers it should be, and the head-teacher may have his views, so may the professional association and other organisations; finally, the teacher has his views. In pointing to the usefulness of this notion of role-set, Merton says: "It raises the general problem of identifying the social mechanisms which serve to articulate the expectations of those in the role-set so that the occupant of a status is confronted with less conflict than would obtain if these mechanisms were not at work" (Merton, *op. cit.*, p. 111).

It is one of the merits of Radcliffe-Brown's writings that he has laid emphasis on the relationships between social positions. The term he used, and which has gained a wide currency, is *social structure*. The structure of any entity is the formal arrangement of its parts, as when we speak of the structure of a building or the structure of an organism. Radcliffe-Brown asserted that the elements of a social structure were persons, but it is more satisfactory to regard them as positions that persons occupy, as at times, indeed, he seems to do. The important point is that structures persist apart from particular persons in the sense that a position may at one time be occupied by one person and at another time by another person. Social structure, then, is a term which permits us to consider continuity. We speak of a school or a regiment or a club as each having a continuing and substantial identity although the persons occupying the positions in these structures change over time.

Morover, there is a relationship between the parts in a structure. Thus the sociologist may be interested in the positions of father, mother, son, and daughter because he wants to know something about the mutual expectations people occupying these positions have; he will accordingly be concerned with the *social organisation* of the family or with the *social structure* of kinship relations. Or again, he may be interested in the positions of director, manager, supervisor, shop assistant, in which case we expect him to be concerned with the social organisation of a department store or the structure of working relations. It is because social positions are organised in certain ways that the sociologist is often led to regard them as *systems* as well as structures. We must examine the advantages of this further.

To begin with let us be aware of what we have been doing. We have been considering certain aspects of human behaviour. It is obvious that we can only at one time consider a few aspects, for the complexity of human behaviour is so great that it escapes our understanding. We have, in other words, been abstracting from reality, and to help us we have selected some general aspects rather than others from the whole of reality. We denote them by use of certain terms, but the use of these terms is now rendered rather more precise than probably would be the case in their common everyday use. Furthermore, we choose to study the relationships between these aspects of behaviour and we find it profitable to suppose that if one aspect of behaviour was to be altered that it would lead to an alteration in other aspects. It is for this reason that it is found useful to speak of a *social system*. In doing so we are making use of a model that is familiar to us, applying it to the other analytic terms we wish to use.

Social Systems

The term system has a variety of applications, for we speak of a hydraulic system, an electrical system, we apply it to organic phenomena as when we refer to the nervous system, and just as a jurist speaks of a legal system or an economist of the banking system so the sociologist also makes use of it in discussing social phenomena. Systems have certain properties in common, in particular that the parts are so structurally related to one another that a change in one part affects the others. In a social organisation like the family, we know full well that a change in the behaviour of one member affects the others. Similarly, in considering a structure of social positions where roles are played in terms of a related body of norms we speak of an institution like kinship as having the properties of a system.

Now sometimes the sociologist regards a society, like an African tribal society, for instance, or even a large-scale modern industrial nation, as a total social system. We shall have to ask how far he is justified in doing this, but we may note at once that in so doing he usually means something different from what we have been considering so far. A department store or a family is an organisation of people whose relationships are systematically ordered or arranged. We may abstract and study the systematic relationships between kinship positions, but when we consider kinship as an institution we are thinking of systematically related norms governing role-playing; institutionalised behaviour, in other words.

The sociologist who is interested in total social systems is investigating the relationships between these institutional structures, which are sub-systems of the total social system. He is looking, for example, at the relationships between the legal, political, economic, religious, and educational structures. The point we are making is that the units of the system are different in each case. What we have, then, is merely a general guide to help us in description and analysis. We may consider aspects of social behaviour as being systematically related, we may speak of a society as being a social system, we may investigate the relationships of sub-systems to the total social system, but we must always be aware of the nature of the elements or the unit members of the system under investigation.

These theoretical formulations are guides, their value rests on how far they prove to be useful. There are, to be sure, many problems connected with theoretical formulations such as we have been describing, some of which are discussed by Firth (1954 and 1955), Emmet (1958), Parsons (1949), and Merton (1949); but although we cannot dispense with them we must be always ready to modify them to suit our purposes.

It will be clear from what has been said so far that sociology does not concern itself with individual people, although, of course, it recognises that society is no more than a number of people, nor does it concern itself with all their behaviour, but only with behaviour that is socially standardised, that is to say which is of a type and which is governed by social norms; in other words, institutionalised behaviour. Any form of behaviour constituting a role or role-set appropriate to a social position is institutionalised in terms of a body of norms, and where a set of norms govern a number of actions we speak of a *social institution*. There is a set of norms governing those forms of behaviour which lead to a man and a woman being married; marriage, then, is a social institution; others include property, law, science, and so forth. It follows that whilst social institutions refer to a complex of roles they are a higher order unit (Parsons, 1952, p. 38). It is important not to confuse units belonging to different levels of analysis or, as philosophers say, to make a category mistake.

Functional Analysis

If we are thinking in terms of social systems composed of social institutions we are led to ask: What do social institutions do? Or rather: What does this particular social institution do in relation to the whole system? The sociologist argues that it performs a function or functions, and seeks to see how these functions contribute to the whole system to maintain it as an on-going concern. This notion of function raises many problems which have been very ably discussed by Emmet (1958). She argues that the notion of function is applicable where:

(a) the object of the study is considered to form a system taken as a unitary whole;

(b) which must be so ordered as a differentiated complex that it is possible to speak of part-whole relationships;

(c) and the parts are elements which can be shown to contribute to fulfilling the purpose for which the whole has been set up, or if it has not been purposefully set up, to maintaining it in a persisting or enduring state. (p. 46.)

At first sight we may readily see a distinction between *purpose* and *function*, but on closer inspection we may perceive something of the connotation of purpose in the use of the term function, for we are saying more than that a social institution *x* has the result *y*, and this because we are speaking about a unitary system with an enduring structure. As Emmet says: "This assumption of an ordered context means that if we say that *x* has a function, we are, in fact, saying more than that *x* has the consequence *y*. It has the consequence *y* within a system the efficiency or maintenance of which depends (*inter alia*) on *y*" (Emmet, *op. cit.*, p. 47). We are concerned with the contribution of a part to the maintenance of the whole, and whilst this is quite satisfactory we must not let it lead us to make assumptions which are dubious. As Emmet points out, in biology the concept of function has provided a way of speaking about organisms as self-maintaining, on-going systems in an environment, without postulating any conscious purpose or design. The danger is perhaps that sociologists may not do justice to conscious purpose on the one hand and may over-emphasise the unitary and integrated properties of societies on the other. But there are cases where the elements of a social system may be said to act functionally for the whole system, and it is these that are of particular interest to the sociologist.

Let us briefly add that if we are able to point to an element and say it is functional for the system, this cannot mean that its existence as an element is thus justified, desirable, or indispensable, nor, for that matter, can we evaluate the system of which it is an element. We can and must avoid introducing value judgments of this kind into our analyses. In fact, it cannot be too strongly asserted that we must avoid assuming that functions are good, for we are defining them only in terms of their contribution whereby with respect to any social system we see them as enabling it to persist or endure. What persists *may* not, according to moral or ethical criteria, be held to be desirable, but such criteria cannot be derived directly from this kind of study. Headhunting in Borneo *may* possibly serve a social function, it *may* independently be held to be an undesirable practice. It *may*, however, be the case that pig-sticking will act as a substitute serving the same function, but whether this or headhunting is or is not a desirable practice, or one relatively more desirable than the other, is something the sociologist cannot decide; nor can he, apart from independently-acquired ethical criteria, say anything about the value of the society in which these things take place.

The tendency for functional analysis to be used, or rather mis-used, to support either conservative or radical social philosophies and policies has been pointed out by Merton (1949), but neither the one nor the other tendency is inherent in this kind of sociological analysis. Indeed, the principal advantage of considering institu-tions in terms of their functions is that it helps the sociologist to carry out objective investigations, that is to say, it enables him to avoid referring to the subjective intentions and aims of people, or at least it helps him to avoid necessarily doing so.

Human purposes may be directed to many ends. They may be oriented to the end that a society be enabled to endure as such, but much more likely they will be oriented to individual or sectional ends. Some purposes, however, may be identical with functions. To make the distinction between those that are and those that are not, Merton (1949, p. 51) in emphasising the distinction introduced the terms *manifest* and *latent* functions. He defines them as follows : —

> "*Manifest functions* are those objective consequences con-tributing to the adjustment or adaptation of the system which are intended and recognised by participants in the system.
>
> "*Latent functions*, correlatively, being those which are neither intended nor recognised."

A well-known illustration of the difference is the case of the periodic ceremonies held by the Hopi Indians, the manifest function of which is that by ritual action of a certain kind rain may be induced to fall. The sociologist argues that there is a latent function in such ritual ceremonies, for they bring together the members of a scattered tribe. Thus assembled, and engaging in common ritual activity, the group's identity is reinforced.

Finally, it must be pointed out, lest we assume that social systems or sub-systems are more highly integrated than they are, that some elements may be *dysfunctional*, or functional in one respect whilst being dysfunctional in another. That it is functional for an economy with full employment and labour scarcity for mothers of young children to go out to work does not mean that it is not dysfunctional for the well-being of their children.

Having outlined the general theoretical orientation of much modern sociological investigation, we shall cease to be so abstruse and proceed to show in what ways it has been found to be helpful. In the next chapter an illustration is given of the ways in which some of these concepts are used and what kinds of conclusions may be drawn from the analysis. The model of a system is applied on two levels, that of structures of positions and roles and that of systems of institutions within a total social system. In subsequent chapters we shall be discussing both simple non-literate societies and modern urban industrial society, and we shall discuss them at both levels. It will be seen that much of the investigation into simple societies is in terms of social institutions, whilst much of the study of modern industrial society is in terms of structures of social positions and roles within institutional sub-systems.

BIBLIOGRAPHY AND FURTHER READING

Banton, M., *Roles: an introduction to the Study of Social Relations,* 1965 (Tavistock).

Davis, K., *Human Society,* 1948 (Macmillan, New York).

Emmet, D., *Function, Purpose, and Powers,* 1958 (Macmillan and Co.).

Firth, R., "Social Organisation and Social Change", *Journal of the Royal Anthropological Institute,* 84, 1954.

"Some Principles of Social Organisation", *Journal of the Royal Anthropological Institute,* 85, 1955.

Johnson, H. M., *Sociology: a systematic introduction,* 1961 (Routledge and Kegan Paul).

Merton, R. K., *Social Theory and Social Structure,* 1949, Rev. Ed. 1957 (Free Press). *On Theoretical Sociology* (1967). Paperback.

"The Role-set: Problems in Sociological Theory", *British Journal of Sociology,* VIII, 2, 1957.

Mitchell, G. D. (Edit.), *A Dictionary of Sociology,* 1968 (Routledge and Kegan Paul).

Nadel, S. F., *Anthropology and Modern Life,* 1953 (Australian National Univ.).

Parsons, T., *Essays in Sociological Theory, Pure and Applied,* 1949, Rev. Ed. 1954 (Free Press).

The Social System, 1952 (Tavistock).

CHAPTER III

A RURAL SOCIAL SYSTEM

In order to illustrate what we have been considering, that is, to show how sociologists find it useful to conceive of societies as systems, we take as our example the work of C. M. Arensberg and S. T. Kimball (1940), a pre-war work which describes a rural community in Eire, and we shall refer also to a slightly earlier account of the same study of the Irish countryside by Arensberg (1937). Our reasons for selecting this topic are, in the first place, that it well illustrates the theoretical approach we have described, but, secondly, it is interesting in that, whilst the investigators used for the most part social anthropological methods of study, they applied them to the study of a community in Europe, and thus the subject matter is perhaps less unfamiliar than that of a primitive society might be. Moreover, it is a study that deals with problems which are reasonably close to us; problems of public policy and administration. For many of the social problems of rural Eire can be seen in modified form elsewhere in the British Isles, as described by Mitchell (1950 and 1951), Williams (1956), Saville (1957), and Frankenberg (1957).

The rural community which Arensberg and Kimball wrote about is situated in County Clare in the west of Eire; a county which, as regards its agriculture, is fairly representative of the country. Farms are, broadly speaking, of two kinds: the larger type of farm where the land is used almost entirely for raising cattle, only a small plot being set apart for a kitchen garden, and where agricultural labour is hired; and the small type of farm engaging in mixed farming, producing for both the market and family consumption, and utilising the labour of the farmer's family. The large type of farm is usually about 200 acres or more, the small type of farm about 50 acres in size. In Clare, small farms are in the majority, as, indeed, over Ireland generally, and it is this unit that is of particular interest to the sociologist.

The Farm Family

The small farm is usually a continuous plot of land, on which stands the farmhouse, and the members of the farm family thus spend most of their lives and perform almost all of their work within this area containing land and house. A study of the social life of this rural community might begin with a reference to economic or demographic matters, but sociological reasons, which will become apparent as we proceed, lead us to begin with the farm family.

Let us, then, consider the structure of social positions and roles. There is the farmer, his wife, and their children. Distinctions are made on the basis of sex and age, and these distinctions govern not merely the division of labour but the whole field of a person's behaviour. The farmer, as we might expect, directs the farm policy, carries out the main tasks of cultivation, and cares for the stock. Wherever heavy manual work is required he is responsible for it. He buys and sells cattle, sheep, and pigs, disposes of produce, and is responsible for the decisions as to how income should be spent. The wife is responsible for the housework, raising children, raising, too, calves and all young stock, keeping chickens, occasional work in the fields, milking cows, making butter and cheese, and so forth. The income from the sale of eggs, poultry, and butter is usually hers to dispose of. But both the husband and wife must use the income they receive in the interests of the farm and their family.

So rigidly are the duties divided that it seems, to the country-folk, almost as if the division is a natural one based on the different aptitudes of the sexes. The children do little except run the occasional errand until they are six or seven, when they take their First Communion, but from that time they progressively take on more tasks; albeit they are tasks differentiated according to their sex. Even whilst at school a boy may be brought home to help with the farm work, and when he leaves school he will usually engage in it full time. Sons do not get paid for their labour, and should they take on part-time work off the farm they hand their earnings over to the father. The relationship between father and son is one of super- and sub-ordination; parental authority and filial obedience bound together by mutual respect. Children are referred to as "boy" or "girl", terms indicating their social positions;

and they continue to be so called until they cease to be under
parental control, as on their marriage or when the father dies.
This appellation takes no account of physical growth or maturity
for it reflects a social distinction, and a man of forty-five may still
be called a "boy", that being his social position. It is an ascribed
position.

Kinship

Outside the family there are relations with kinsfolk. It is here
that the farm family is primarily articulated with the wider community, for there is much mutual assistance given, for which no
payment is made, between people in the local community, and it
takes place mostly between kinsfolk. The nature of this co-operation may take the form of lending tools, farm equipment, or working
on another's land at spring sowing or ploughing, the lending of a
"boy" for turf-making or at harvest, the pooling by women of their
resources in butter-making, sending a girl to help in the house,
generally assisting at times of distress, and participating in ceremonies like funerals and so forth. Such co-operation is known
locally as *cooring*. It represents the obligation that one has to
one's kinsfolk, described by the Irish as "friends", but it also
extends to neighbours. The closeness of the kinship relationship
determines largely the degree to which a "friend" has a "call" on
one's assistance. Hence, socio-economic relationships are based
to a very great extent on kinship relationships. It is worthwhile
to look at the latter more closely.

Strictly speaking, the small farm family is bilateral. Descent
is reckoned through both parents, but with an emphasis on the
father's family. A man normally inherits from his father, and just
as he takes his father's name (patronymy) so the farm also is known
by the family name; farm and family are closely identified. In
Clare a man's friends are his father's relatives, and he will speak
of "close" or "distant" friends, not in terms of their geographical
placement but in terms of their degree of relationship to him.
And as might be expected a person feels he has a more pressing
duty to help close friends than distant ones. One interesting feature
of kinship relations is that the terms used to describe kinsfolk are
descriptive rather than *classificatory*, that is to say, as compared
with the English custom (which is still mainly descriptive), the

Irish more often avoid the terms "nephew" or "grandson", preferring to speak of "brother's son" or "son's son"; although the term "cousin" is used it is much more usual to speak of such a person as one's friend, and if he is one's father's cousin to refer to him as "my father's friend".

Now just as there is a diminishing sense of obligation to kinsfolk the more distant they are, so there is an intensification of the taboo on marriage the closer they are. Although the Church places an impediment on marriage of cousins, even to the fourth degree (*i.e.* third cousins), it does grant dispensations, but it is felt even when they are granted that there is something anomalous in cousins marrying, although it not infrequently occurs. Again, the practice of *cooring* extends to one's mother's kin, but not to those who are not of blood relationship, that is to say, not to those who have married into her father's family. Similarly, one has obligations to one's wife's friends and at the same time they are brought within the bounds of the prohibited group.

More or less, this is the kind of kinship system that we are familiar with in Europe and America, but there are some minor variations, and there is a certain definiteness and extension of relationships that is unusual. We do not usually have much to do with cousins, very seldom with second cousins, but in the Irish countryside these kinsfolk may be important, for, depending on one's position in the community, mutual obligations of a social and economic kind may be not inconsiderable.

Marriage

Marriage is an important institution in most societies, but in the Irish countryside and in the small farm family, in particular, it has a decisive and far-reaching effect on the lives of many folk. There is no custom of primogeniture or junior right, but the farm descends to one son and the father has the choice as to which it shall be, and, moreover, when he shall take it over. Always the transfer of the farm to the chosen son is on the occasion of the son's marriage, but the latter's marriage is only to a small extent in the hands of the couple getting married.

Marriages take place when a satisfactory match is made. It is held to be desirable for the bride to come from another farm family of approximately equal position in the community, and discussion often takes place among kindred as to who would be a suitable person. Suitability is defined primarily in terms of what serves the interests of the farm. Many things are taken into account, not the least being the size of the dowry she will bring with her. For the amount of the dowry is of material concern to the parents of the boy and, possibly, to other members of the family, for it may furnish a dowry for a daughter marrying out.

On the marriage of the son the land is transferred and the old couple retire, although they usually continue to live on the farm. Arensberg tells of the arrangements customarily made for their well-being and the place such old people occupy in the community (1937). A legal agreement combining marriage settlement and transfer of land is drawn up in which provision is made for the retiring couple, and when this is done and the marriage solemnised the rest of the family must disperse. There is a change in social positions and in consequence a change in relationships as roles alter.

The process of adjustment is very often a difficult one; it could hardly be otherwise, but it is rendered easier than one might suppose by the existence of a body of custom, tradition, and folk-lore surrounding the changes; behaviour in new circumstances is institutionalised and the means are at hand for making a relatively smooth adaptation. If in the new dispensation there is strife between the mother and the daughter-in-law, then, when it becomes intolerable, custom decrees that it is the old folk who must go, but such cases are rare. On the other hand, there is a strong pressure on the young couple to produce an heir, and a woman's lot is hard if she should fail to do so.

The practice of the "country divorce", as it is known, has not altogether disappeared. Although a man is forbidden to divorce his wife and marry again, a man whose wife does not bear children may, if he has a brother, hand over the farm to his brother on condition that he marries, but a monetary payment will be made by way of compensation. Formerly, a man who gave up his farm might send his wife back to her parents. Thus we see there is a very high value placed on preserving the farm family as a structural unit and the name of the farm.

At times of birth, marriage, or death, friends gather (sometimes those who have emigrated from the countryside to the town or abroad come home) and the identity of the family and the link between the family and the farm are reaffirmed. Here we are pointing to a body of sentiments shared and expressed; this is but the psychological counterpart of the sociological facts we have been outlining.

What we have, then, is a system of social positions, roles played according to well-established norms, a pattern of institutionalised behaviour centring round kinship, the system of land tenure, the agricultural economy of the small farm, and the institution of marriage. It may seem that much is lost by casting this description in what appear to be the "bloodless categories" of sociology, but our purpose is not to tell a story but to understand certain aspects of human behaviour, to try to appreciate the nature of the social system of this rural society, and by this means to see if we can shed some light on the social problems facing the policy-maker and administrator; it is to this that we now turn.

Emigration: A Problem Requiring Explanation

One of the problems that interested Arensberg and Kimball was the remarkable drainage of able-bodied people from the countryside, and indeed from the country as a whole. Emigration is something that has come to be associated with the Irish, for many have found their way to America in the past and still large numbers come annually to the United Kingdom in search of employment. Let us see what the authors have to say on the subject.

The investigation was carried out in the early nineteen-thirties and the authors had to rely for demographic facts on the census of 1926. The picture presented was of a country possessing an abnormally high proportion of elderly people, most of these being in the rural areas rather than the towns. In Clare there were 752 people between sixty-five and seventy-four years of age in the rural areas as against 528 in the urban areas. This disproportion is a feature of Eire. To be sure it is sometimes found elsewhere, for instance in parts of England, where it is largely to be attributed to mechanisation of agriculture and the consequent reduction in the demand for labour (Mitchell, *op. cit.*), but this was not the case in Eire when this subject was being investigated.

Furthermore, the authors discovered some interesting facts about the proportions of the sexes. Thus there are many more men than women in the countryside, and there are many unmarried people. Indeed, one of the striking facts about Eire is the late age of marriage; we are told that no other country keeping records shows a larger proportion of unmarried persons of all ages. The authors give the following figures taken from the census, which are expressed here in tabular form:

TABLE I

Age Group	Percentage Unmarried Men	Percentage Unmarried Women
25-30 years	80	62
30-35 ,,	62	42
35-40 ,,	50	32
50-65 ,,	26	24

These are very high percentages, the significance of which may best be appreciated if we compare them with figures in other countries, particularly Denmark, which is also predominantly an agricultural country, at about the same time.

TABLE II

Age Group	England and Wales		Denmark	
	Percentage Unmarried		Percentage Unmarried	
	Men	Women	Men	Women
25-30 years	45	41	49	39
30-35 ,,	25	26	25	25
35-40 ,,	16	20	15	19
55-65 ,,	10	15	8	14

Thus we have a remarkable case of late marriage and a high incidence of bachelorhood, and it is more pronounced in the rural than in the urban areas of the country. For instance, in Clare, we are told that 88 per cent. of the males between twenty-five and thirty years of age were unmarried, whilst in some other counties, like Sligo, Galway, and Mayo, it was 90 per cent. or more.

Now these facts call for some explanation, and an explanation that will take into account the small farm family, for it can be statistically demonstrated that no other occupational class delays marriage so long. Furthermore, there is in Eire a very high incidence of fertility among women, but even so there is, as compared with other countries, a normal proportion of children under fifteen years of age. In other words, few and late marriages balance the high fertility rate to maintain a normal number of children.

This statistical picture is illuminated when we look at it in the light of our sociological analysis, for marriage brings about a dispersal of the farm family. Hence, in order to maintain structural continuity and so permit the social process to endure, families have periodically to be reconstituted and in such manner that the farm is adequately worked. Unmarried children leave the farm. Some may marry a girl into another farm, very occasionally a boy into another farm if there is no son to inherit it, but most leave for the towns. Some who leave the district may take up shopkeeping, particularly if the father has some capital to help a son set himself up; some, of course, have already been trained for other kinds of work such as the professions or the priesthood, but these we are not concerned with for they will have left before the transfer of the farm. For many the only choice is to emigrate. But we may well ask: Why does it happen in this way? Why must there be late marriage and bachelorhood? We must in answering point to the consequences of the kinds of relationships existing within the farm family: the authoritarian relationship that the parents have toward their children and their reluctance to give up control of the farm until they are well advanced in years. But beyond this we can point to the self-sufficiency of the family, the close bonds tying the members together in a common enterprise, and their strong identification with the patrilocal plot of land. These, again, are psychological counterparts to our sociological analysis, for they represent elements of the personality system that corresponds to this kind of social system.

Thus far we have focused attention on the structure of social positions and roles within the farm family, but we have also referred to kinship and marriage, which are two of the most prominent social institutions in this society. There are, however, other institutions which should be mentioned.

Other Institutional Aspects

Briefly, we should point to the differentiations made on the basis of age and generation, whereby people of similar age form habitual associations in cliques or groups. Arensberg and Kimball have much to say of interest about the influence in the local community of groups of old men who meet to debate and discuss local matters.

Then there is the local division of labour, a system of communal services, some of which are remunerated by a money payment, some of which are not paid for but are offered in the same manner as *cooring*. There are numerous people, many being small farmers, who tend to specialise in some way: one is an amateur veterinary, another a bonesetter, one is a pig killer, whilst another is skilled in rigging hayricks, and all these and many other handymen do odd jobs for people. To be sure, there are skilled craftsmen and tradesmen, and these tend to mix judiciously work for which payment is made in money and help to local people who may respond more often than not with gifts or manual assistance. Such an organisation of labour and skills unites people in the community, it marks off the local community from those who live outside it and who are paid for their services, as they also pay for services rendered them, and it is also a means of establishing equivalences of worth, that is social worth, or what we may call *social status*.

Again, there is the set of relationships between members of the community and those in the towns and the markets where farm produce and animals are sold. Here there are many customary forms governing the distribution and sale of goods and many instances of ceremonial and ritual in bargaining and effecting purchase and sale. All this is very ably described by the authors with a wealth of detail and illustration that cannot be mentioned here.

Now what we have very briefly described represents systems of institutionalised behaviour, and it is not difficult to see how they are articulated one with another to make up the total social system. If we are interested in some aspect of the countryman's life we may well find it necessary in giving an account of it and in proffering an explanation to refer to these sub-systems which appear to mutually reinforce each other.

Applied Sociology

It is the chief merit of the study we are considering that the authors point to the implications of their analysis for policy-making. Such a social system as this is so structured as to provide strong resistances to social changes.

An attempt to alter an institutional pattern may very well unexpectedly encounter powerful resistances because of the interrelationships between the parts. Consider the concern expressed in Eire at continuous emigration, declining population, and the high incidence of bachelorhood. It is a process that has gone on for a long time and still continues. It is a phenomenon that is usually accounted for in terms of poverty, the attraction of employment abroad, and scant industrialisation at home.

Now these may well be factors which should be taken into account in explaining it. Doubtless there are "pulls" from abroad as well as "pushes" from at home, but it is surely very inadequate to describe the "push" as caused solely by rural poverty. As the authors say: "The argument is the familiar argument. The phenomenon is conceived only as an economic one. Human action is merely the pursuance of economic goals. In this case, the argument runs specifically, the matter is the result of poverty. Since the conditions persist, it is a matter of 'endemic' poverty. One has only to change the cause, do away with the poverty, and all else will right itself" (1940, p. 315). Such a view, they point out, is quite inadequate, both because it rests on too narrow a view of human motivation and because it ignores important sociological factors. It is these latter that we are concerned to indicate, and the way we have done so is to describe the society as a system, discerning the sub-systems of institutional behaviour, investigating the nature of systems of social positions and the roles corresponding to them, and perceiving relationships between the parts by the help of these analytical tools.

In this case our analysis has drawn attention to kinship and marriage especially and the system of positions and roles in the small farm family. In doing so we have discerned some of the latent as well as the manifest functions of social institutions, and, in particular, the latent function of emigration. For emigration is no new phenomenon; the history of it over the years is largely the story of the process whereby it has become institutionalised, and to-day we may glimpse ways in which emigrating members of a family give assistance to other kinsfolk, how dowries are earned by girls in England to enable them to return and take up the honoured position of farmer's wife, and, in short, how the practice enables the *familistic* rural system to persist. It is difficult to see, if emigration was to be prevented, how this kind of small farm family could persist. We may hazard the suggestion that should emigration be stopped, the character of the entire rural society would be changed.

Let us conclude by saying that in endeavouring to discern the latent functions of institutions we have a means of understanding much in the social fabric of this rural society. Such an understanding does not tell us what the policy-maker should do, but it does provide him with a means for more fully appreciating the nature of his problems, and this is the practical import of our discipline.

BIBLIOGRAPHY AND FURTHER READING

Arensberg, C. M., *The Irish Countryman*, 1937 (Macmillan and Co.).

Arensberg, C. M., and Kimball, S. T., *Family and Community in Ireland*, 1940 (Harvard).

Frankenberg, R., *Village on the Border*, 1957 (Cohen and West), and *Communities in Britain*, 1966 (Penguin).

Littlejohn, J., *Westrigg*, 1963 (Routledge and Kegan Paul).

Mitchell, G. D., "Depopulation and Rural Social Structure", *Sociological Review*, XLII, 4, 1950.

"The Relevance of Group Dynamics to Rural Planning Problems", *Sociological Review*, XLIII, 1, 1951.

Saville, J., *Rural Depopulation in England and Wales, 1851-1951*, 1957 (Routledge and Kegan Paul).

Williams, W. M., *The Sociology of an English Village: Gosforth*, 1956 (Routledge and Kegan Paul).

A West Country Village, Ashworthy: Family, Kinship and Land, 1963 (Routledge and Kegan Paul).

PART II
THE PRINCIPAL SOCIAL INSTITUTIONS OF THE SIMPLE SOCIETY

CHAPTER IV

KINSHIP AND MARRIAGE

In the early days of sociology people spoke of *primitive* societies, and they used this term largely because they assumed that what was so described represented an early stage in the evolutionary process; *primitive* was then contrasted with *modern*. The distinction is an interesting one, for whilst we need not make the evolutionary assumption, it is worth comparing and contrasting types of societies. Indeed, a long line of sociologists have made what is basically the same distinction, as when Spencer distinguished between *militant* and *industrial* societies, or Durkheim between *mechanical* and *organic*, or Tönnies between *Gemeinschaft* and *Gesellschaft*, or MacIver following him between *community* and *association*, or Maine between societies based on *status* and societies based on *contract*, or Giddings' distinction between *ethnic* and *demotic*, and more recently Redfield's distinction of *folk-culture* and *civilisation*. We are referring, of course, to two broad types of society.

The Simple Society

The type which interests us in this section we call the *simple society*. We describe it so because it is relatively simple in social structure, it is relatively less differentiated than our own urban industrial type, it has no great division of labour, usually its economy is of a subsistence kind, it is relatively highly integrated, and has a propensity to persist unchanged in structure; Redfield has identified such as peasant societies (1956). Now, all this is true of our rural Irish community, a contemporary society in western Europe; but other simple societies studied by modern sociologists (who usually call themselves social anthropologists) are also contemporary ones, such as, for instance, those in Africa.

The description "simple" rather than "primitive" is chosen because it helps us to avoid the suggestion that these are merely historical relics of an unprogressive past. The fact is that we study these contemporary societies partly because they are easily observable and can thus be studied more scientifically than historical

ones, but also because, being less enthralled by the idea of progress than earlier sociologists, we find it profitable to discover
alternative kinds of social organisation; alternative means to the
end of enabling people to live in harmony. We may, indeed, learn
much to our profit from investigating these varied forms of social
organisation; at least after serious study we shall be less inclined
to say of them: "Habits beastly, manners none."

In simple societies there are two features that stand out. One
is the large part played by those social norms we usually call custom,
for the members of this kind of society have a common knowledge
of a large body of custom. They do not have to refer to legal
experts or to written records of rules and regulations in the same
way or to the same degree as we do in the complex modern society
in which we live; customs regulate social behaviour extensively.
The second feature is that to a large extent this body of custom is
closely related to kinship. We saw quite clearly in the Irish study
that kinship was a pivot around which revolved a host of rights,
duties, expectations, and action; indeed, kinship organisation is by
far its most important aspect. This is frequently even more noticeable when we turn to study other simple, often non-literate, societies
found scattered all over the world. We shall, in fact, find that
kinship is a most important subject for study, for it tells us a lot
about the way a simple society is organised. Such a study shows
us, in fact, how important ascribed social positions are in this kind
of society. To begin with, however, it is useful to look at some of
the customs governing relations between kin.

Customs of Joking and Avoidance

We have already, of course, noted a case of mutual assistance
amongst kinsmen practised according to custom; but there are other
and less easily understood customs which are widespread; two such
related ones are the highly conventionalised practices known as
joking and *avoidance*.

A. R. Radcliffe-Brown pointed to the existence of such standardised forms of behaviour in Africa, Oceania, Australia, and
North America. In most cases they appear to be usages regulating
the behaviour of people related by kinship or marriage. Thus permitted disrespect obtains between brothers-in-law, or between a
nephew and his maternal uncle, or between a man and his wife's

sisters. In Radcliffe-Brown's words it "is a relation between two persons in which one is by custom permitted, and in some instances required, to tease or make fun of the other, who in turn is required to take no offence" (1940, 1952, p. 90). It may be mutual, as when each person makes fun of the other, or asymmetrical as when a nephew makes fun of his mother's brother, but the latter cannot respond in like manner. The relationship is, according to Radcliffe-Brown, a peculiar combination of friendliness and antagonism; it is of such a kind that were it to take place in any other social context it would arouse hostility.

Often age determines whether such behaviour will take place, for a man may joke or play the fool with his wife's younger brothers and sisters but not with her older ones. What is particularly interesting is that frequently this conventional form of behaviour is found together with one which appears very different, namely that of avoidance by one person of another. Usually this is the avoidance by a son-in-law of his wife's parents, and especially of his wife's mother. He may not look at her, use her name or a word suggestive of her name. Now this might look like hostility, but it is clearly meant to be an expression of respect. A typical instance is described by Peristiany with respect to the Kipsigis of Kenya: "Whenever a man meets his mother-in-law, he must change his direction, so that they may not find themselves face to face. If he desires to speak to her, he must address her from some distance, and he cannot eat food cooked by her or enter her hut . . ." (1939, p. 106).

It is useful to consider both types of behaviour together. Thus Radcliffe-Brown has argued that marriage brings together two different families; there is detachment of a wife from her family and attachment to her husband's, what he describes as social disjunction and social conjunction, for there is, as regards the former, a divergence of interests between a man and his wife's parents and, as regards the latter, a bringing together of families. The one presents the possibility of conflict and hostility and the other implies the undesirability of strife.

To maintain the mutual respect necessary contact is restricted; it is one way of dealing with the situation. But the same kind of situation may arise with regard to other people, such as between a man and his wife's brothers and sisters. Here another way of dealing with the situation is to indulge in mock hostility, playful antagonism, and horseplay, which calls forth by custom a similar light-heartedness and thus expresses a basic friendship. Sometimes this may occur before a man is married, for in some societies marriage is preferred between a man and his mother's brother's daughter. Where this type of marriage is esteemed the sons and daughters of a man's maternal uncle, who are described as his cross-cousins, have a joking-relationship with him. Apart from these instances there is also a similar relationship between clans or tribes sometimes, as described by Fortes of the Tallensi (1945), but the explanation given seems adequate to cover these cases also.

These relationships of joking and avoidance, calling forth symbolic conventional behaviour, have been mentioned because they are clearly governed by custom. It is custom that decrees the kinds of people involved, the circumstances, and the times when this behaviour is appropriate. There are many other customs governing behaviour between kin and between kinship groups, some of which we shall refer to, but in order to understand them it is necessary to examine kinship in some detail.

Kinship Relationships

When we use the term *kinship* we are referring to people who are related by consanguinity and affinity. Now the focal point of our attention is the elementary family of parents and children. In our own society this two-generation family is an easily identifiable unit. We may include grandparents, uncles, aunts, nephews, and nieces, and if we do we have covered for the most part the kin who are recognised. In other societies, however, the family itself may well include some or all of these, but also more distant kin than these. Moreover, there may be more than one wife (polygyny), occasionally more than one husband (polyandry). Such compound or extended families are not uncommon in many simple societies; indeed, their simplicity may seem to be belied by the complexity of the kinship pattern, although this is usually the only sphere in which there is much complexity.

One of the first things to note about kinship is that it constitutes a system of relationships. There is, as Radcliffe-Brown says, an assumption being made when we speak of kinship systems, namely that there is a complex relation of interdependence between the members. According to the nature of this interdependence, so kinship systems differ according to type. There are a number of variables to be considered. In the first place, descent may be reckoned either through the father's family or through the mother's family or through both with varying emphasis. If it is through the father's family we speak of patrilineal descent, if through the mother's of matrilineal descent. Secondly, on marriage a wife may move to reside with her husband or a man may move to reside in the locality of his wife and her family, when we speak respectively of virilocal and uxorilocal residence, or it may alternate periodically, as in the case of the Dobu described by Fortune (1934). In the third place, property and rank may be inherited either through the male line or the female line, or both. Lastly, the authority over members of the family may be in the hands of the father and his family or it may be in the hands of the mother's family, in which case it is usually exercised by her brother.

If all these variables incline toward the father and his family we may speak of a patriarchal kinship system, if to the mother's family of a matriarchal one. But it is not infrequently the case, indeed it is usually so, that there is a mixture. Thus, for instance, there may be in a particular society bilateral descent with an emphasis on the female line, virilocal residence with inheritance from both, and a division of authority. In fact, most peoples are bilateral, recognising both the male and the female lines for various purposes. However, descent plays a large part in the organisation of relationships and influences behaviour in far-reaching ways, so we must examine it more closely.

In the elementary family there are social positions of father, mother, and children. This means that there are three sets of relationships: those obtaining between parents, between children, and between parents and children. These may be called relationships of the first order. If we consider two such families related to each other through one member we have relationships of the second order. A further link with another family, such as with father's brother's son, gives us relationships of the third order, and so forth. In our society only a very restricted number of relationships based on kinship and affinity are used as the basis for social organisation, but in many societies relationships of the fourth or fifth order may be used extensively as a basis for organising behaviour of an economic, political, or ritual nature.

This might at first sight seem a very cumbersome method, for clearly a man may have a very large number of relationships of the fourth or fifth order, and he usually does. But when we examine the genealogies of families we note that relatives are classified. Thus only a few terms may be used to describe relatives. A man may not only use the term "father" for his own father, but he may extend its use to describe other men; he may not only refer to his two grandmothers by a term that we would translate by the term "grandmother", but he may extend its use to refer to many women irrespective of their age and generation. Thus a few kinship terms used to distinguish lineal relatives are also used to refer to collateral relatives such as cousins; sometimes a term like "brother-in-law" is used to refer to people linked to a man through marriage who are quite distantly related to him.

All this may appear rather odd, but we have to realise that our way of reckoning descent is not the only way in which it may be done, and that in society where kinship plays an important part our system may be quite inadequate. The interesting thing to note is that this practice of classifying relatives occurs in both patrilineal and matrilineal kinship systems. Moreover, if we compare instances of the two we shall find that there are many similarities; similarities which are a result of the utilisation of the same principles. It is one of Radcliffe-Brown's major contributions that by comparative studies of kinship systems some of these principles of classifying kinship systems have been detected, and we shall briefly outline what he has said about them (1950, Intro., and 1952, Chap. 3).

Structural Principles of Kinship

Siblings, that is to say, children of the same parents, usually display a measure of solidarity, but as well as this well-known phenomenon of sibling solidarity Radcliffe-Brown pointed to the unity such a sibling group has in relation to a person outside the group but connected to it through a relationship with one member. Thus a group of brothers and sisters constitute a unit in relation to the son of one of them who is related but outside their group. This *unity of the sibling group* is reflected in the kinship nomenclature involved. Thus, in Fig. 1, *A, C,* and *E* are brothers, whilst *B* and *D* are their sisters; Ego is the son of one of the brothers. Now whilst in all societies sex is a basis for distinguishing social positions in a kinship system, seniority also forms a similar basis, although more weight is given to it in some than in others. In those societies where it plays little part, Ego may refer to the men of this sibling group by the same term he uses for the one who is his father, and in important respects his behaviour towards them is similar to that which he adopts towards his father. In the same manner, in a sibling group where one of the women is his mother he will refer to the other woman by the same term he uses to refer to her. Moreover, his father's sisters, too, are addressed by a similar nomenclature, and so are his mother's brothers. In some societies even sex as a differentiating factor is subordinated to the principle of the unity of the sibling group, for Ego may refer to his father's sister by a

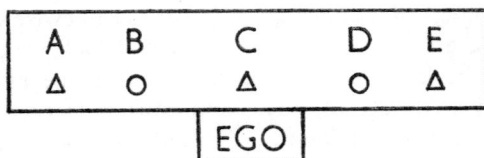

FIG. 1.*

term which may be translated as "female father", or his mother's brother by a term which may be translated as "male mother".

That this should seem strange to us is because we place the emphasis on physiological differences, whereas in such kinship systems as we are considering the distinctions are sociological ones, or as it is sometimes said *jural* ones; that is to say, the nomenclature denotes the kind of behaviour that is binding on a person and which he must adopt towards people with whom he is linked in the system of kinship relationships. The obverse of this is found in some societies where a man has the same term for his own children and those of his brother, but these children are addressed by another kinship term by their mothers and their mothers' brothers and sisters. Thus unity of the sibling group is preserved, but unity in the sense that they constitute a group or class towards the members of which an individual related to one of them is bound

* Figs. 1, 2, and 3 are reproduced by permission of the Royal Anthropological Institute from "The Study of Kinship Systems" by A. R. Radcliffe-Brown, *J. Roy, Anth. Inst.* LXXI, 1941. Fig. 1 has been slightly altered in the interest of clarity.

by the same kinds of behaviour. Of course, there is some difference in behaviour according to sex and age, but basically it is much the same. To his father Ego adopts a restrained and respectful manner; he extends it to his father's brothers and his father's sisters. To his mother Ego is more affectionate, and he has with her a less restrained relationship; this is extended to her sisters and also to her brothers.

It is perhaps not surprising that very often there is a joking relationship between a man and his mother's brother, a relationship which would be impossible between him and his father's brother. By the same token it is not surprising that often a man has a relationship of avoidance with his father's sister. Kinship nomenclature is thus a clue to our understanding of social behaviour.

This principle also operates with regard to other sibling groups, so that the siblings of a man's grandfather are likewise classified as belonging to a group with the members of which he displays the same kind of basic behaviour. But, of course, the principle may be applied in a variety of ways, and thus it is that systems of different types are to be found. Although it does not provide a sufficient explanation, this principle does give us a clue to understanding the existence of such customs as the preferred marriage of a man with two or more sisters, technically known as *sororal polygyny*; marriage of a man with his deceased wife's sister, known as the *sororate*; marriage of a woman to two or more brothers, known as *adelphic polyandry*; and marriage of a man to his brother's widow, known as the *levirate*.

Another principle that Radcliffe-Brown propounded on the basis of comparative studies of kinship systems is the *unity of lineages*. By a lineage is meant all the descendants of a man through at least three generations. If it is a patrilineal lineage it will be through males, sometimes known as an agnatic lineage, if matrilineal through females. A lineage group consists of all members alive at a given time. Now by speaking of the unity of the lineage group he indicated the manner in which a lineage group formed a single entity *vis-à-vis* a person linked to it by kinship or affinity. Distinctions are made on the basis of sex, age, and so forth, but there is a basically common relationship to all the members of the lineage which is reflected in the kinship nomenclature and expressed in behaviour.

In illustrating this Radcliffe-Brown chose to compare two North American Indian tribes: the Fox Indians, who have been studied by Sol Tax (1937), and the Hopi Indians, who have been studied by Eggan (1950); the former tribe is patrilineal and the latter matrilineal. The point of this comparison is that the same principle is seen to be operative in both cases. It is instructive to consider this illustration. Thus the Fox Indians use a kinship terminology similar to our own, describing the appropriate people as father, mother, brother, sister, grandfather, grandmother, father's sister, and so forth,

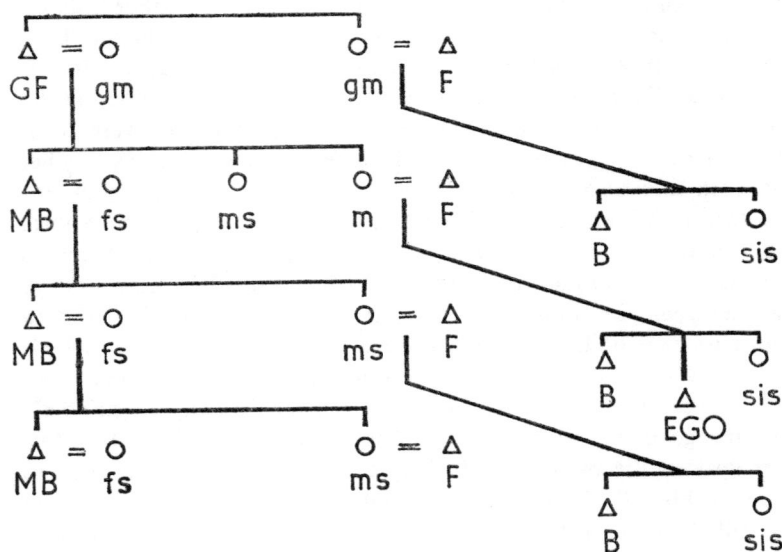

FIG. 2. FOX INDIANS—*Mother's Lineage.*

although we see the principle of unity of the sibling group illustrated in the case of the sisters of a man's paternal grandmother, for they too are called "grandmother". Yet, when we look at a man's mother's lineage, *which is not his own*, we see clearly the operation of the principle of lineage unity, as set out in Fig. 2. Here, apart from Ego's mother's father, properly described as "grandfather", the men of the lineage through three generations are described by a term meaning "mother's brother" and the women of his own and junior generation as "mother's sister". Men marrying into this lineage are all called "father", one of them being his own father, and the children of all the women of this lineage are called "brother" or "sister".

If we look at a man's father's mother's lineage, which again, of course, is not his own, we see the same principle applied, for the women are all called "grandmother", one of them being his own, and the men are called "grandfather". Again, it is the same with respect to the wife's lineage, although the men, apart from his wife's father, are called "brother-in-law" and the women "sister-in-law", irrespective of age and generation. In his wife's mother's lineage the women are all called "mother-in-law" and men "father-in-law".

Now turning to the Hopi Indians a man's lineage is his mother's and he distinguishes the women members of her lineage, with one exception, in a familiar manner as grandmother, mother, sister, niece; the exception being the niece's child, who is referred to as "grandchild". Among the men he refers to his mother's brother as such and also his nephew as such, but he calls his mother's mother's brother and his sister's daughter's son by the same term that he uses for his brother; the significance of this we shall return to later. A classificatory term of "sister-in-law" is used for all women marrying into the lineage, and he includes all the children born to men of his mother's lineage in the same category as his own children, calling them by the same term. When, however, we look at the father's lineage, which is not Ego's own, the principle of lineage unity appears again quite clearly (Fig. 3). Over five generations the men are called by the same term that he uses to address his father. With the exception of his father's mother, who is called "grandmother", the women are called "father's sister", whilst the men they marry are all classed as "grandfather". Similarly, the women marrying the men of this lineage are called "mother". The father's father is called "grandfather", but the principle of lineage unity is not seen to operate with regard to this lineage for the reason that among the Hopi a man is not regarded as being related to his father's father's lineage at all. But the principle does operate with regard to the mother's father's lineage, where the women are called "grandmother" and the men "grandfather".

Radcliffe-Brown argued for a further structural principle which he called the *unity of alternate generations*. This is based on observations that members of alternate generations seem frequently to be on easy, unrestrained, and friendly terms with one another.

Sometimes the system of kinship nomenclature is such that men of alternate generations are called by the same term, a term that may be translated as "grandfather" or, sometimes, as "brother"; in the latter case age and seniority are recognised by the prefix "older" or "younger".

This phenomenon of alternate generations of men being identified has been seen in the case of the Hopi man's mother's lineage,

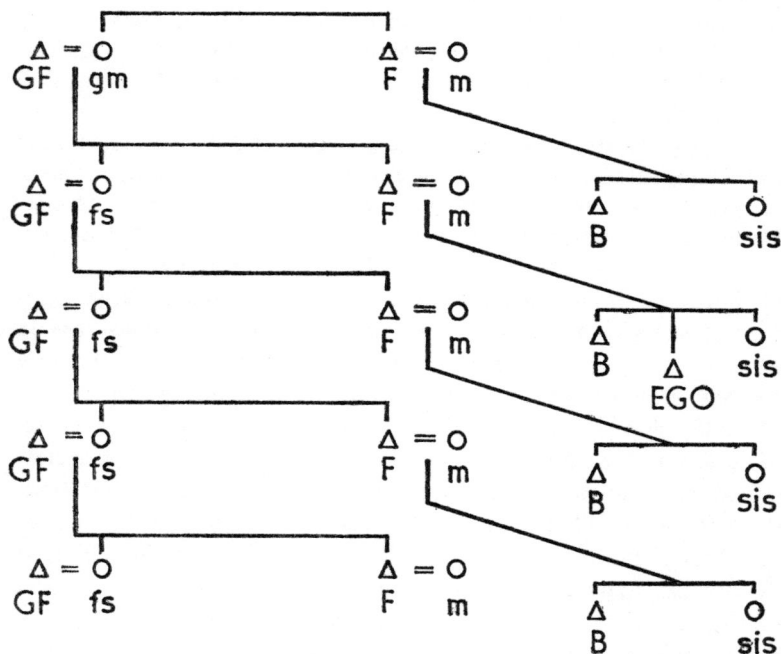

Fig. 3. Hopi Indians—*Father's Lineage.*

in which his mother's mother's brother and his sister's daughter's son are referred to by the same term as he uses to describe his brother. In fact, quite a number of kin are often called "grandfather", and the nomenclature seems to indicate that with them a man is on terms of ease and friendliness, whilst to a man's classificatory father's sisters, of whom there may be a considerable number, he is on very respectful, but also correspondingly restrained, terms.

Some societies organise kin in clans.* A clan is a larger group than a lineage, but is thought of in much the same way. In fact, clan members are not always related by kinship, but they suppose that they are. It has been observed that sometimes clans as a whole are regarded as units, so that in a matrilineal society all the men of a man's father's father's clan may be called by the term "grandfather" and the women "grandmother", and he will possibly be expected to seek a wife from among his classificatory grandmothers. The Tallensi, described by Fortes (1945), are a society organised in clans, and the greater part of the description of their social system must necessarily be concerned with clan structure and relationships. Many, although by no means all, of the simple societies of North America, Australia, Asia, and Africa are divided into clans, as, of course, were the Scots as vestigial remains indicate.

Now in the light of this kind of analysis of kinship nomenclature we are better able to understand the institution of marriage. Clearly, marriage involves sets of kin, it alters the content of relationships, it imposes obligations, and so forth. Where large numbers of kin are involved its regulation is a matter of considerable importance. In the case of kinship systems like that of the Fox Indians, a man having married a woman of one lineage enters into a relationship to that lineage as a whole; his wife's sisters are, therefore, in a relationship to him which Radcliffe-Brown has described as *quasi-marital*, and it involves no great upset of relationships if he should, before or after his wife's death, marry one of her sisters. For already his and his wife's children and her children by another marriage will be regarded as belonging to the same kinship category. Here we have a case of sororal polygyny. A psychologist may well point out that co-wives who are sisters are more likely to live together amicably than if they are unrelated, and that a stepmother is more likely to show affection for her sister's children than another woman's, but these arguments Radcliffe-Brown has pointed out merely reinforce the sociological argument he puts forward.

It is clear that kinship systems differ, and in the case of unilineal descent systems there is a world of difference between the two sets of kin a man has, his mother's and his father's kinsfolk, and

* American anthropologists often refer to them as *sibs*.

accordingly his rights and duties towards them. However, a word of caution is needed, for it must not be supposed that the kinship terminology accurately reflects the distribution of rights and duties. Indeed, Professor Fox (1967) has gone to some pains to show that there is often only a rough and ready correlation between the terminology and the rights and duties. Some writers like Lévi-Strauss (1949) argue that the terminology serves to classify people into "marriageable" and "unmarriageable" people. Thus in one system persons are forbidden to marry anyone to whom they apply a kinship term, whilst in another a person may be obliged to choose a marriage partner from among those persons to whom a special kinship term is applied. There is, in fact, a realm of controversy here which we cannot go into but merely indicate. Professor Fox himself believes it is better to view kinship terminologies as ways in which people classify their kinship universe, and of course we should remember that kinship may occupy most of a person's social universe as it tends to do among the Australian aboriginal peoples. He goes on to say that this may indeed be an ideal classification and not one which corresponds very closely to "real" groups. What is important is to examine such terminologies so that we may discern the manner in which a people see themselves and their social organisation. Some of their distinctions may be very significant, as between maternal and paternal uncles for instance, whereas this distinction for a European may be unimportant.

The Incest Taboo

Let us now turn to another aspect of kinship, namely the widespread but somewhat variable rules regarding incest. This topic is selected partly because it has been frequently studied but also because it illustrates a very important principle of sociological enquiry. This is the necessity to beware thinking too rigidly in categories drawn from our experience in our own type of society.

Some traditional or simple societies have customs prescribing preferred marriages, sometimes marriages of people who are kinsfolk, but there are other customs that proscribe not only marriage but sexual relationships with various classes of kinsfolk and others not related either by blood or marriage. Lowie cites the

case of an Australian of the Emu group in one tribe who is forbidden to marry a woman of the Emu group in another tribe,
although they are separated by over a hundred miles and are quite
unrelated (1921, Chap. 1). Sanctions applied against offenders vary
in severity, but are often such as to emphasise the seriousness with
which infringements are regarded; incest, indeed, is strongly
abhorred. So great is the horror it arouses that some have thought
aversion to incest to be instinctive, but we need not assume this to
be so.

In all societies sexual relationships must be controlled, not
merely because strong passions are involved, but because it is
important that children are placed in responsible hands and their
upbringing safeguarded. If there are means for caring for children
born out of wedlock, then, other things being equal, a measure of
sexual promiscuity may be allowed, or this may occur where abor-
tions or infanticide are practised. But there is no society which
does not regulate human reproduction in some way, and it is
arising from this that among other controls there is an incest taboo;
a taboo that appears to be universal.

It would seem that at the core of the prohibition is the need to
legitimise children, to assign them without ambiguity to a family,
although, of course, the size and composition of the family may
vary greatly from one society to another. A moment's reflection
will show how the incest taboo is essential for the well-being of the
family as an organisation, for incest between members of a family
would render social positions and roles extremely ambiguous. It is
not merely that it would promote sexual rivalry between siblings,
leading to the possibility of fratricide, or between parent and child
with all the attendant dangers of jealousy, but the rights and duties
that are part and parcel of the social positions of parents and
children would be disrupted. As Davis has pointed out, an
"incestuous child of a father-daughter union, for example, would
be a brother of his own mother, and at the same time a son of
his own sister, a step-son of his own grandmother; possibly a brother
of his own uncle; certainly a grandson of his own father. This
confusion of generations would be contrary to the authoritarian
relations so essential to the fulfilment of parental duties" (1948,
p. 403).

Incest and Adultery

It will be noted that incestuous relationships involving a married person are also adulterous, and recent work on this subject has focused attention on the importance of examining both phenomena together. Yet we might profitably ask, firstly, how we are defining these terms, for in the English language we usually think of incest as consisting of sexual offences with members of one's near kin by blood and marriage, whilst adultery is regarded as an offence between a married person of opposite sex outside that marriage. In our own society incest is a punishable offence, in fact, a crime, whilst adultery, although reprobated, is not.

J. R. Goody (1956), in a comparative study of two West African peoples, the Ashanti and the Tallensi, has shown how misleading it can be to use the terms we are familiar with in analysing practices in other societies. The Ashanti are a matrilineal people who make a distinction between tribal and household sexual offences; the former require adjudication by the central authority of the tribe whilst the latter are settled in a more private manner. Tribal offences include sexual relations between a man and woman of the same matri-clan, for which the offenders are executed. They also include offences by a man with a woman of his patrilineal sub-group, including father-daughter offences, and these are punished by death or by expulsion from the matri-clan; but these two, whilst distinguished, may be classed together as calling forth the extreme penalty. The second type of offence, falling into the household category, is between a man and a wife of a member of his descent group or other classificatory wives, and here the penalty is a payment. An offence with any other married woman is likewise punished by a fine. It is interesting to note that the Ashanti distinguish between parent-daughter incest and brother-sister incest, but the major distinction they make is between what may be called *intra-group* offences and *group-wife* offences.

The Tallensi are a patrilineal people and do not appear to have a word corresponding to "incest". Nevertheless, they do distinguish between classes of behaviour and differentiate them according to their seriousness. Thus the Tallensi seem to make a distinction between offences committed by a man with a member of the same patri-clan, such as with a paternal aunt, daughter, or sister, which are thought to be thoroughly disreputable acts, and offences

committed by a man with the wife of a member of the same patri-
clan, such as the wife of a father, brother, or son, and these offences
are thought of with all the repugnance we associate with incestuous
relationships and against which public opinion among the Tallensi
reacts strongly. There is a further type of behaviour which is
disapproved of, namely sexual relationships between a man and the
wife of a non-clansman.

Now the interesting feature of this comparison is that both the
Ashanti and the Tallensi distinguish intra-group offences from
group-wife offences and both from offences between unrelated
persons. Goody suggests that it is the same for other societies
characterised by unilineal descent. Now among the patrilineal
Tallensi intra-group offences, such as those between brother and
sister, are regarded as reprehensible whilst group-wife offences are
regarded with extreme horror. Among the matrilineal Ashanti the
reverse seems to be the case, for the intra-group offences are
punished by death whilst group-wife offences are treated as a more
serious form of extra-clan adultery and are settled by a payment.

The reason for these differences is not far to seek. In a patrilineal society like the Tallensi wives are of fundamental importance
to the clan for through them its continuity is preserved, and offences
by a man with a wife of another member are serious. In a matrilineal society like the Ashanti descent is through females, and
offences with sisters are therefore heinous for they derogate their
position in the kinship system. Goody points to the interesting
feature that in neither society does the father-daughter offence fall
into the most heinous class, but mother-son offences do. By way of
explanation he says: "In the Tallensi the mother is the closest
wife of a clansman of senior generation, while in the Ashanti she
is the closest *female clan member* of senior generation" (p. 296).
Or, expressed in other words, he points to the fact that in patrilineal societies the rights over a woman that are transferred at
marriage include both sexual and reproductive rights, whereas
in matrilineal societies it is only the sexual rights that are transferred, and these not necessarily exclusively.

Kinship as an Organising Basis for Social Life

So far in this chapter we have concentrated on kinship and
marriage and some of the customs connected with these social

institutions. The importance of kinship, it has been indicated, lies in the fact that it provides a basis for social organisation. It is instructive to look at some of the activities for which kinship does serve this end. All people must work to live, but the manner in which a livelihood is obtained can vary greatly. Yet we find that kinship plays a big part in the economic organisation of life in the simpler societies. Not infrequently the family is the basic unit and husband and wife both have their tasks to perform, with assistance from older children, more distant kin helping from time to time; or for some purposes quite a large body of kin may gather. In cases where there is an extended or compound family, again we have numbers of kin organised for economic activity.

It is not always the case that co-operative efforts are limited to kin, but kinship units, from elementary families to sub-clans, provide the organisational structure for such activities. Most peoples engage in some form of agriculture, although they may, in addition, hunt and fish. There is division of labour to a variable extent, seldom very much, but occasionally we find specialisation occurring, as when a man sets himself up as worker in metal or wood or makes pottery and so forth; but very often these are supplementary activities undertaken by some members of the family as and when the need arises.

A brief consideration of some African societies shows us different kinds of economies. Among the Bantu peoples the BaBemba, for example, described by Richards (1939), engage in shifting agriculture, cultivating plots of land for a time and then abandoning them for others. They practice the rotation of crops and grow millet, maize, pumpkins, beans, peas, groundnuts, and manioc. Plots are cultivated by families, land is fairly plentiful, and there is no need for the village headman to allocate land, a practice that obtains in the more southern Bantu tribes. There are occasional gatherings of people for hunting expeditions and for fishing drives. Among the Tonga of Northern Rhodesia, described by Colson (1951), women cultivate fields of their own which their husbands clear and plough. The men tend the cattle, an exclusively male occupation. Parties of people occasionally gather for hunting, less so to-day than in times past. The Nyakyusa of Tanganyika, described by G. Wilson (1951), are given to polygamous marriages, and among them each wife has her own fields, which her husband will hoe with the help of his sons, but which she plants, weeds, and harvests with the help of her children. She provides and cooks food thus grown for her husband and children. Co-wives often help each other, but have no rights over each other's plots or produce, although in return for help cooked meals are provided.

Moving from Africa and looking at the small Polynesian island where the Tikopia live, of whom Firth (1936) has provided a very good description, we find a complicated system of land tenure. Land is scarce and property is distributed to families and clans in small plots scattered round the coastal strip of the island. These plots of land are cultivated as orchards, producing breadfruit, paper mulberry, Tahitian chestnut, coconut, sago, and bananas, or as gardens for producing taro and yams. Land may be divided up on the death of the head of the family, sons obtaining their own, but sometimes several brothers may share under the aegis of the eldest. Women have an interest in their father's land, and may pass it on to their children for one generation. Thus, lands are held on a family and kinship basis, but there are wide rights of temporary use and, in fact, if any man is hungry he may help himself to a neighbour's coconuts or breadfruit, although good manners will dictate that he tell him afterwards and possibly give him a present. Oddly enough, a man may plant taro on another's land without permission, although when he goes to collect the crop he will make a gift to the owner or be agreeable to some similar return arrangement at a later date.

Property Relations

Short as is this reference to kinship and economy, it has soon brought us to the subject of property, for kinship is the main basis not only for the production but also for the transference of property. Of course, simple societies seldom have very much in the way of permanent property apart from land. Though they have highly developed political organisation, the Barotse people of Central Africa have few possessions and one man lives as well as another, despite great differences in rank. This is because in Central Africa it is almost impossible to store food or keep goods for any length of time; heat, moisture, destructive insects, and flooding all combine to keep personal property to a minimum. On the other hand, we should not forget such African people as the Kipsigis and the

Masai who keep large herds of cattle. However, in speaking about property we may include non-material items in our definition, such as rank, ritual privileges, and magical knowledge.

In order to illustrate some of the features of the holding and transfer of property let us briefly describe the institution as seen among the Kipsigis, and in this example see how property and kinship may be related. The Kipsigis, as we have mentioned, keep cattle, and they prize them highly, but they also engage in agriculture to provide them with food; yet the cattle provide meat, milk, and blood, which is also used as a food, whilst at the same time serving other social functions such as conferring social esteem and providing the means for effecting marriages.

Land for cultivation is not individually appropriated, but may be individually possessed. The produce of the fields associated with each family is stored for the use of that family, each polygamous wife having her own, but the husband has his own fields, the produce from which he uses to entertain his friends. In addition to this "field of the house" that the wife has, there is usually a small vegetable garden cultivated entirely by her and used for her needs and those of her family. As land is plentiful little value is attached to it.

The property that is important to the Kipsigis is their cattle. Cattle fall into three categories: those cattle a man obtains from his own efforts, formerly looted after raids on his enemies; those he inherits from kinsfolk; and marriage cattle. Cattle in the first category a man may dispose of as he likes and he may kill them for food or otherwise use them as he pleases, except that custom decrees that he will give cattle as gifts or on loan to others from time to time, and there is a widespread distribution amongst fellow tribesmen which redounds to the prestige of the donor. Marriage cattle are those given by a man to his father-in-law after the marriage with his daughter, and these are regarded as the property of the woman's brothers by the same mother. A man is obliged to keep these cattle for his sons by that wife until they are grown up and they, in their turn, require cattle for the bridewealth that is part of the exchange that cements the marriage. What a man does with his daughter's marriage cattle is strictly controlled, so that he cannot sell them or kill them for meat, except in a few and pressing circumstances. In effect, such cattle belong to the man's sons.

When a man dies his eldest son by his first wife and his eldest son by his second wife, who undertake the burial arrangements, may select a given number of beasts from their father's herd together with certain of his personal effects. The rest of the man's property is divided equally between all his "huts", *i.e.* his polygamous wives' families who normally live separately, irrespective of the number of children in each family, but this distribution may be spread over a number of years. Immediately after the man's death the eldest son of the first wife takes charge of the herd, distributing it as and when necessary. Married sons may claim their share immediately, but unmarried ones receive their share of cattle when they need it for bridewealth on the occasion of the marriage. Daughters receive no cattle, for cattle must be kept in the clan, so that besides being patrilineal the Kipsigis also restrict inheritance to the agnatic line, although widows receive sufficient to support them and their children. The father may not will his property as he wants, although he may express some wishes, and these more often than not are carried out. It is likely that the dying man will urge his sons not to exact full repayment for cattle loaned to other men, so that the goodwill of friends toward him is not destroyed at his death.

In the simple society we may see a variety of rights, and sometimes they can be quite complicated. Frequently, they are connected with kinship, but in some societies with an elaborate political system, like the Zulu or the Swazi, property may be held on an almost feudal basis; this, says Lowie (1921), is particularly so of the Dahomey of Uganda, where the king was owner of the land and in theory disposed of it at will. But rights may, in addition to land or cattle, include non-corporeal rights over the use of magic formulae, as among the Dobu of New Guinea, and these may be inherited. In fact, one may find societies where magic is inherited in the male line whilst more concrete property is inherited in the female line.

Respect is maintained for copyright even, for among the people of the Andaman Islands a person composing a song owns it in the sense that no one but he would dream of singing it. Both individual and collective control over property is found in simple societies; the weighting varies. In one society the whole of a man's estate is automatically divided on his death according to customary law, whilst in another society a man may will his property almost as he pleases, and, indeed, he may disinherit his nearest kinsfolk, although this is rarely found in extreme form. Usually property is kept within the kinship unit, and if the society is clan-structured it is very likely to remain within the clan.

Finally, although we cannot dwell on this, we should note that marriage is to a large extent a matter of transferring rights over persons, the rights over the woman being married and also over her children yet to be born. The transfer is not from one person, a father, to another person, a husband, but from one kinship group to another. Here the social institutions of kinship, marriage, and property are subtly related. As Phillips, Mair, and Harries (1953) have pointed out, we should not too readily assume, as some writers in the past have done, that marriage is often in such societies a simple matter of economic exchange or purchase.

BIBLIOGRAPHY AND FURTHER READING

Colson, Elizabeth, "The Plateau Tonga of Northern Rhodesia", *Seven Tribes of British Central Africa*, Eds. E. Colson and Max Gluckman, 1951 (O.U.P.).

Davis, Kingsley, *Human Society*, 1948 (Macmillan, New York).

Eggan, Fred., *Social Organisation of the Western Pueblos*, 1950 (Chicago).

Firth, R., *We, the Tikopia*, 1936 (Allen and Unwin).

Fortes, M., *The Dynamics of Clanship among the Tallensi*, 1945 (O.U.P.).

Fortune, R. F., *Sorcerers of Dobu*, 1934 (Routledge).

Fox, Robin, *Kinship and Marriage*, 1967 (Penguin).

Goody, J., "A Comparative Approach to Incest and Adultery", *British Journal of Sociology*, VII, 4, 1956.

Lévi-Strauss, C., *Les structures élémentaires de la parenté*, 1949 (Presses Universitaires).

Lowie, R., *Primitive Society*, 1921 (Liveright).

Peristiany, J. G., *The Social Institutions of the Kipsigis*, 1939 (Routledge).

Phillips, A., Mair, L., and Harries, L., *Survey of African Marriage and Family Life*, 1953 (O.U.P.).

Radcliffe-Brown, A. R., "On Joking Relationship", *Africa* XIII, 3, 1940; reprinted in A. R. Radcliffe-Brown, *Structure and Function in Primitive Society*, 1952 (Cohen and West).

Radcliffe-Brown, A. R., and Forde, Daryll, Eds., *African Systems of Kinship and Marriage*, 1950 (O.U.P.).

Redfield, R., *Peasant Society and Culture: an anthropological approach to civilization*, 1956 (Chicago).

Richards, A. I., *Land, Labour, and Diet in Northern Rhodesia*, 1939 (O.U.P.).

Tax, Sol, "The Social Organisation of the Fox Indians", *Social Anthropology of the North American Tribes*, Ed. F. Eggan, 1937, Rev. Ed. 1955 (Chicago).

Wilson, G., "The Nyakyusa of South-Western Tanganyika", *Seven Tribes of British Central Africa*, Eds. E. Colson and Max Gluckman, 1951 (O.U.P.).

CHAPTER V

LAW AND POLITICAL SYSTEMS

Law and Order

In our modern industrial society we all have some knowledge of the law, but what we know is only a small part of the whole of it. This is because the law is vast in its content and highly specialised. In fact, we need not be aware of, for instance, mercantile law unless we are engaged in international trade, nor is there any necessity to be versatile in the law relating to contract or tort or conveyancing, and so forth. It may be that from time to time we are required to know something about these aspects of the law, but then we usually consult a specialist in law; we see a solicitor. However, we all know something about criminal law; the law forbidding theft, fraud, murder, and so forth. If we look for law in simple societies we may not find it in a very recognisable form, nor may we easily detect people specialising in it. Yet, on the other hand, we may among some non-literate peoples discover the existence of courts in which evidence is taken and judicial decisions are made, perhaps with appeals to higher judicial bodies.

To say anything of a general nature about law and about political arrangements in simple societies is not at all easy. There are, indeed, many similarities and many differences, and all that we can do here is to note some of the main ones. When we discuss law and politics we are concerned with the means for maintaining order. In the simple society, as we have already seen, kinship is a social institution helping to maintain social order, for the simple society is undifferentiated compared with our own, which has specialised institutions for this purpose. Thus, if in any particular society we fail to find clearly developed legal and political organisations, we should examine its kinship system to see in what ways it replaces them. Social order, then, is our point of departure. But first we must define our terms.

Folkways and Mores

We have previously referred to norms and, more specifically, to custom, but there are several kinds of norms to be distinguished, of which customs constitute only one kind. Customs may be differentiated into *folkways* and *mores*. Sociologists usually speak of folkways to describe the norms governing patterns of everyday behaviour. They are norms defining role-playing, and so familiar are they that we are often unconscious of them. They are the norms that determine the standardised use of language, eating habits, greetings, and so forth; in a word, they govern appropriate behaviour. Deviations from this kind of norm are corrected by such social controls as ridicule, mild ostracism, and gossip. We may infringe a few such norms and perhaps be regarded merely as eccentric, but if we persist in doing so, or infringe many, then informal social sanctions will be brought to bear on us designed to bring us back into line with our fellows. In simple societies these sanctions are rather more powerful and the folkways thus more rigid than in our own society, which, being so differentiated in structure, permits some variety in the patterns of folkways.

Mores are norms which are regarded as much more important, indeed essential, to social welfare. In our society mores govern such relationships as those between doctor and patient, priest and parishioner, and other professional relationships; they uphold pre-marital chastity and post-marital fidelity, and so forth. The sanctions that are brought to bear on those who infringe mores are thus stronger and severer than in the case of folkways. In the simple society they are extremely important, and sanctions may be very severe, as in the case of a man being banished from the circle of kinship and tribe.

The Ubiquity of Law

Besides folkways and mores there are laws, which are usually enacted by a legislature and enforced by a politically-governed executive in whom authority is invested. Law is precise and sets out in detail the nature of the norm. Law can be known either because it is enacted and written down or else, if not enacted, because appeal is made to the judicial decisions that have set precedents. Similarly, the sanctions brought to bear on an offender are known or can be known.

It has sometimes been thought that law is a pre-requisite for social order, and early travellers among simple peoples, seeing that law was absent, were apt to conclude that the stability of such societies was precarious. The question whether such societies do have law or not depends on our definition of law. Some societies, such as the Zulu or the Barotse in Africa, some of the Polynesian societies, and some American Indian tribes like the Omaha, have or did have judicial organisations for dealing with offenders and for settling disputes between people; that is to say, they have courts or tribunals with recognised judges. Nevertheless, some societies do not display these things, or they have seemingly an ephemeral, vague, or ill-defined mode of maintaining order; of these, we may say they have no law because these societies are not politically organised. We shall return to discuss political organisation later. Let us pause to ask if the absence of law, defined in terms of judicial institutions, means that such societies are less well ordered than those that do have it.

Malinowski, impressed with the extent to which simple societies were ordered and unimpressed by many contemporary and ill-informed views about what were called savage peoples, drew on his experiences of field-work in Melanesia to illustrate the nature of primitive law (1926). The absence of law defined in terms of "central authority, codes, courts, and constables" does not, he argued, mean that there is an automatic submission to custom. Sometimes men in simple societies break the rules, but the observance, generally, of such rules is neither the result of the fear of punishment nor of a general submission to all tradition, but rather it is the result of a complexity of factors; it is these that Malinowski tried to illustrate.

Much of what he does is to offer psychological explanations in terms of motivation. Thus, in economic exchange, for example, the distribution of a catch of fishes by coastal dwellers to inland villagers and the reverse movement of vegetables, there is an underlying motive of self-interest governing the customary rules involved which defines the behaviour of the people concerned. Widows, by custom, mourn their husbands, publicly displaying their grief. Doubtless the grief is real, but added is the motive that the husband's kin are more likely to support the widow if she shows respect for him than if she does not do so.

Malinowski is at pains to show by his one example how society is made up of a complex of relationships, that the very interaction between people generates the interests that support the customary ways of behaving, and that herein lies the source of stability. Later sociologists, like Homans (1951) and Klein (1956), interested in small groups, have endeavoured to show in more abstract terms the relationships between interaction, sentiments, and norms, and how social control emerges.

Malinowski was anxious to enlarge the concept of law, to do justice to the facts as he observed them, and point to the stability that a simple society may possess. But he also wanted to separate unconsciously obeyed custom from the more specific requirements laid on mankind. "There must be in all societies", he says, "a class of rules too practical to be backed up by religious sanctions, too burdensome to be left to mere goodwill, too personally vital to individuals to be enforced by any abstract agency. This is the domain of legal rules, and I venture to foretell that reciprocity, systematic incidence, publicity, and ambition will be found to be the main factors in the binding machinery of primitive law" (p. 68). But we need not quibble about the definition of law, it is more important to see how order is maintained in a society, for clearly there may well be a high degree of stability where, strictly speaking, there are no legal institutions.

Social Control

It is a widespread practice in simple societies for kinship groups to control and defend their members. If a man suffers a loss or injury his kin are involved. They seek compensation from the offender. If one of their number is killed they must be compensated for his loss, and they usually obtain it under threat of vengeance; custom lays down the amount of compensation, as in the ancient *weregild* of Anglo-Saxon times. Thus, whilst kinship provides the organisation for the settlement of disputes there is a body of custom governing the process. The Ifugao present an instance where disputes are settled on a kinship basis, but it is interesting to note that two parties to a dispute may choose a go-between unrelated to both of them. Yet his power is only limited to his ability to persuade. Communal settlement and opinion seem to hold the ring in a dispute and may well oblige the opposing groups to come to amicable agreement; at least there are customary limits to the extent to which sets of kin may fight each other.

In our society we make a broad distinction between civil and criminal law, but to seek a similar division in simple societies is misleading. A better distinction is between what Radcliffe-Brown has called "public" and "private" delicts. Thus personal injuries are often settled by kinsfolk and may include cases of theft, murder, wounding, and so forth, and these are private matters. But there are other offences which are dealt with on a public or communal basis, and these include very often offences like incest, sodomy, sacrilege, treason, witchcraft, and sorcery; for these offences the punishment frequently is death.

A private delict, even murder, may be settled by the payment of compensation, but public delicts are injurious to the entire community, they arouse the horror and wrath of all, and there is usually some means of dealing with them. Sometimes there is a local council of elders or a meeting of all initiated men before whom the offender is brought. If the general opinion is that he is guilty he may be executed on the spot, the village headman leading the others in carrying out the sentence. In cases of public delicts the community has suffered damage. The offence has weakened the normative structure according to which men live. As Radcliffe-Brown terms it, the social *euphoria*, or well-being, has been turned into a state of *dysphoria*, and something must be done to restore it (1933). Restoration thus depends on a social act that expresses the abhorrence of people of the offence and the seriousness of keeping the rules; the punishment is thus retributive in character. We may speak of penal sanctions being imposed, but there are other sanctions. Apart from moral sanctions that will make a person aware of the disapproval of his fellows there are also ritual sanctions whereby the miscreant is regarded as ritually unclean until he has undergone ritual purification or expiation of his sin.

Thus even when there is no very clearly formed political organisation capable of sustaining permanent legal institutions, there are, nevertheless, institutional means for dealing with offences. Kinship usually provides the framework for coping with private disputes, even with some offences we should regard as criminal. The local group, perhaps a kinship group, but more often a territorial unit like a village community, may be adequate to deal with more serious offences against the social order.

Much more could be said about societies with diffuse legal arrangements, but before we consider such an instance we shall briefly describe a society that possesses a well-defined political structure and correspondingly a formally organised method of settling disputes; this is the Barotse of Northern Rhodesia. The Barotse have been chosen because the political and legal institutions have been subjected to close scrutiny by M. Gluckman, and the description that follows is taken from his detailed accounts [1951, 1955(a)].

The Barotse Judicial System

The Barotse consist of a variety of peoples, ruled by the dominant Lozi tribe, who have established their kingdom with an elaborate political system. Their policy has been to impose on other tribes only the Lozi laws which relate to national matters. Other tribes are permitted to have their own family law and to decide according to their own customs how, for instance, inheritance disputes should be settled. We shall be concerned with the Lozi system, which since British influence had undergone some modifications. There was then the possibility of appeal from the highest Barotse court to the High Court of Northern Rhodesia in civil matters and to the Provincial Commissioner of the Barotse Province in criminal matters. There was also the right to petition the United Nations Trusteeship Council in political disputes. To-day they are Zambian.

To begin this description reference must be made to some general features of the country. The population of Barotseland, of over quarter of a million, dwells in the flood-plain stretching along the Zambesi River, living in villages, tending small plots of land, herding cattle, engaging in fishing and hunting, and manufacturing in simple fashion most of the things they need. The flooding of the plain imposes the necessity for an annual migration to the villages on the margin, but when the floods subside they return to their own districts and their own land. Although their tools are simple their economy is fairly complex. There is some specialisation and a great deal of trading internally and some externally. The people living on the plain produce cattle, fish, sorghum, maize, and various root-crops, whilst the people in the woodland areas on the margin of the plain exchange for these things their own products of tobacco, cassava, millet, groundnuts, honey, mats, baskets, and all kinds of materials and implements like nets and other gear. Here, as in many parts of Africa, material goods cannot easily be stored or preserved, and as a result there is a large degree of economic equality, but whilst all men enjoy much the same standard of living there are vast differences in rank and position.

The Lozi live in villages and till their land with the usual help that kinsmen give each other. The links with kin are very extensive, so that kinsmen in quite distant villages may be called on for help and to take part in marriage and funeral ceremonies. People who are not kin may be added to those a man is related to in terms of friendly assistance; in fact, pacts of friendship are made by the Lozi with other tribes and their members treated as kin. The Lozi are bilateral in kinship, reckoning their descent in many lines; hence a Lozi man has choice as to which group he will attach himself to. Although he may have as many as eight descent names, one from each great-grandparent, he often uses fewer. The classificatory principle is much in evidence in the nomenclature of kinship, particularly the principle of the unity of the sibling group. There is considerable co-operation and mutual dependence in day-to-day living, and a man has many social relationships of a face-to-face character. Yet these relationships are not limited to kinship and friendship, for they extend politically to his lords and his inferiors; to describe these relationships we must look specifically at the political arrangements of Loziland.

Each village has a headman, who may be a member of the royal family, whence we speak of a royal village, or he may be a commoner. He (or she) is responsible to the king in council. In former times there were two capitals, to-day there are five, but still two of the capitals are pre-eminent. Every village is attached to a capital, and at each capital there is a palace and a council house, which may be a fairly imposing structure. The council, known as the *kuta*, is both a political and a judicial body. The councillors are of three kinds; they are distinguished by the titles attached to the mats on which they sit and the order in which they are placed in the council house. The titles have reference to offices of state and may also have reference to past reigns. In the *kuta* to the right of the ruler's dais sit the most important councillors or *indunas*, including the chief councillor or *Ngambela*, who cannot be a prince eligible for the throne but who nevertheless exercises great power so that people speak of him as "another kind of king". On the left of the dais sit the stewards, divided into seniors and juniors, who are councillors mainly concerned with the royal household. Behind the stewards sit the princes and the consorts of princesses representing their wives. In the council house there are places for clerks, police, royal bandsmen, litigants, suppliants, and witnesses. The senior *indunas* and stewards, together with some members of the royal mat, form another council, but the *Ngambela* and the *Natamoyo*, who is a prince who provides sanctuary, are not members of it. Junior *indunas* and stewards, together with junior members of the royal mat, form another council, known as the *katengo* and which exercises much influence. There is a third small council consisting of the *Ngambela*, the *Natamoyo*, and a number of councillors, and this body meets the king at night, the other two councils meeting by themselves during the daytime.

All three councils, as well as the full *kuta* itself, discuss policy matters, sending messages to and from each other as occasion arises. This organisation of the *kuta* is faithfully reproduced at each capital, but in the king's capital the king and the *Ngambela* are supreme over their opposite numbers in other capitals, and this goes also for the senior councillors.

Besides owing allegiance to the headman of his village and to the prince or princess of the royal village to which he is attached, and the capital with its ruler, ultimately to the king, a Lozi belongs to a political sector. These sectors are not territorial units, and their members may be scattered all over Barotseland. Each sector has its head who is the holder of a senior office at a capital, and under this head are other *indunas* to whom a Lozi acknowledges his allegiance. The councillors of a sector may form a court for hearing cases, or if the dispute concerns men of two sectors a joint court consisting of councillors of both sectors may be formed. These and the full councils at the capitals constitute the official law courts of the land, but any headman, councillor, royal person, or notable may hold a court of his own, as may a senior kinsman, and minor matters should be first considered at these. As courts they have no official standing, but a higher body may refuse to hear a dispute unless it has been discussed by such an informal tribunal. A judgment accepted by all parties is reported to the *Ngambela* and the king, and if there is an appeal it is to the *kuta*.

There are two rulers, one at each of the principal capitals, but the ruler at the second capital is a woman, namely the chief princess. Until recently there was no appeal from one ruler to another. Formerly each capital was a sanctuary for people fleeing from the other. This kind of dual monarchical arrangement is not unique, for the Swazi are ruled by a king in one capital and a queen in another, although among the Swazi, as H. Kuper has shown, there is a nice balance of power between the two rulers (1947).

The king is represented in his *kuta* by councillors and is regarded as standing above it. Only on ceremonial occasions will he appear at its meetings, but all the proceedings are reported to him and decisions made by the *kuta* are confirmed by him. The Lozi may be said to maintain, in the best tradition of constitutional monarchy, that the king must do no wrong, for he acts on advice of councillors who may be sued by any person for injustice or any wrongs suffered at his hands. The king is identified very closely with the land by titles like "great one of the earth", and gives land to those who need it. He is equally identified with the people and may be addressed by the title *Malozi*, which is the name of the nation. His position has mystical as well as political associations, and the graves of past kings, too, provide national shrines with ritual and magical connections.

In the *kuta* the *katengo*, or council of the people, has great influence, and other councils tend to defer to or at least refrain from acting counter to its recommendations. Councils confer and try to reach agreements on proposals which may be put before the king. The king is advised by two women, a princess and a commoner, but he may choose any one in addition. Important matters may be referred to the other capital before the king makes his final decision.

This elaborate political organisation exerts a powerful influence on the society. It is not merely a means of making decisions or settling disputes, says Gluckman, but a means of welding the Barotse into a nation. Titles represent past kings and Lozi history, and the greatness of the nation is thus upheld in people's minds and affections. Because members of the royal family marry commoners, thus maintaining over the generations links with a large number of commoner families, there is a check against a too exclusive royalty. The relationship between a man and the king, too, is a personal one, for from him he derives his land and his well-being, the king being his protector against princes and councillors and his defender against his enemies abroad. Indeed, there is a mass of social relationships of a personal nature, largely face-to-face, between people, both political and kinship relations inter-locking; for the king is "father" of his people and every lord a "father" of those under him, but by the same token every father is a "lord" over his dependants; political titles and kinship terms seem sometimes to be interchangeable. "This multiple membership of diverse groups and in diverse relationships", says Gluckman, "is an important source of quarrels and conflict; but it is equally the basis of internal cohesion in any society" (1955, p. 20).

The quarrels and conflicts are resolved by the legal system as the cohesion is a product of the political system. For the Lozi legal system, whilst it differs in many ways from our own has much in common with it. Procedure in the courts is rather different. There is no counsel, although a man's lord may plead on his behalf, and judges tend to examine the plaintiff and the defendant. Appeal is made to general principles which are fairly flexible, like rights, duties, good evidence, negligence, and reasonableness. But, of course, as we might expect in a society where there is a predomi-nance of face-to-face relationships, the judges often have private knowledge of the people who appear before the courts, and this is not ignored.

Moreover, judges seem to be anxious above all to restore to equilibrium the social relationships that have been ruptured by offences. Justice is sought for, but it is the re-affirmation of the norms of the society, says Gluckman, that judges are mainly con-cerned with, and thus the judges' examination of evidence is evalu-ated at all points according to moral norms. Among the Lozi justice must be done, but the people must also be reconciled to one another.

The Barotse present us with an example of a society having strong central government, legal and political institutions, explicit legal concepts, and much of the legal machinery that we are familiar with. Yet in this same continent of Africa there are other societies which conspicuously lack these features, although in many other ways they appear to be similar. One such society is a Nilotic people called the Nuer, who live in the south of the Sudan, approximately 2,000 miles to the north of the Barotse. These people have been studied by E. E. Evans-Pritchard, who has written extensively about them [1940(a), 1940(b), 1951].

Social Control in Nuerland

The Nuer number about 300,000 folk living in swamp and savannah country on both sides of the Nile river, and are thus a society of about the same size as the Lozi or Barotse. Like most simple societies kinship provides the basis for their day-to-day social organisation. They dwell in villages and hamlets, engaging in agriculture, growing maize, beans, and millet, but regarding themselves chiefly as cattlemen. Cattle play an important part in effecting marriages and in defining the status of children. They also fish, but although game abounds they rarely hunt.

As the Lozi are in the Zambesi floods, so the Nuer are obliged to migrate annually, for during the dry season the savannah is parched and bare of grass. When the rains come and the rivers flood the country during the latter half of the year, they live in their villages on knolls and ridges just above the flooded parts; here they cultivate their ground. But when the dry season begins they move to camps which are centred round water supplies. During this migration village groups may be split up and people may be brought together who before were distantly divided; this has implications for their social organisation, as we shall see later.

This is a tribal society, but without a ruler or any kind of central authority whatsoever. Tribes are divided into segments, which Evans-Pritchard terms: primary, secondary, and tertiary. A tertiary tribal segment comprises a number of village populations. Segments have much the same properties as the tribe itself, for they each possess a name, share common sentiments, and have their own territory; the smaller the tribal segment the more compact is its territory and the greater the interaction among the members.

The interesting feature of this social structure is that tribes and tribal segments are defined in terms of opposition to each other: a tertiary segment in opposition to another tertiary segment of the same secondary segment; a secondary segment in opposition to another, both of the same primary segment. If a man has a quarrel with another his fellows support him; if the two men belong to two tertiary segments of the same secondary segment then only these two segments are involved. But if one man is opposed by another in a different secondary segment, then both secondary segments are involved. Thus, to use Evans-Pritchard's diagrammatic illustration (Fig. 6), when Z^1 fights Y^1, then both Z^1 and Z^2 unite as Y^2, but when Y^1 fights X^1 both Y^1 and Y^2 unite, and so also do X^1 and X^2, so that X and Y are opposed. When X^1 fights tribe A, then X^1, X^2, Y^1, and Y^2 unite as tribe B; one tribe against the other. And when tribe A fights the neighbouring Dinka or the Europeans both tribes unite. A group is a group only in relation to other groups.

The Nuer, we are told, are a proud and touchy people, given to quarrelling and feuds. They will quarrel, for instance, about cattle,

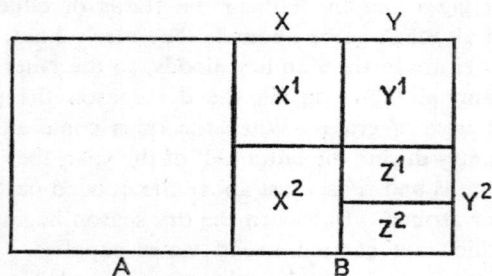

Fig. 6.*

adultery, watering rights, and are quick to discern insults. Their annual migrations which bring many folk into contact with each other aggravate the possibilities for conflicts, yet at the same time making co-operation, or at least peaceful co-existence, more necessary than otherwise. But the only way of settling disputes is by fighting, for there are no courts, no judges, no means of redress of wrongs and injuries except by violence or the threat of violence. Duels between men are common, and if the disputants are members of the same segment they are left to it, but if from different segments their fellows unite to assist them in pursuing their quarrels. Naturally, the dangers of feuding are well known, and this knowledge acts as a check on behaviour that would lead to it, for if a man is killed his kin will demand compensation at least, and they

* Reproduced by permission from *The Nuer* by E. E. Evans-Pritchard, published by the Clarendon Press, Oxford, p. 144.

usually hanker for vengeance. A blood-feud can easily start and spread to become a conflict between larger groups, perhaps lasting a long time. The threat of the feud is powerful in maintaining order.

Nuer are divided into clans, but the clan is not an undifferentiated group of persons recognising common kinship—it is highly structured. The components of a clan are lineages related to each other genealogically, and they may be regarded as possessing a similar character to the structure of tribes, for there are maximal, major, minor, and minimal lineages in a clan. Yet here again it may be said that members form distinct groups only in opposition to each other. Thus a member of a minimal lineage is a member only in opposition to another of the same minimal lineage. Collateral lineages of the same branch will fuse in relation to another collateral lineage. Now, although these lineages are not so many territorial groups they do have associations with localities. A village is associated with a lineage, which may be described as the dominant lineage. Hence a village is a group of persons clustered round an agnatic lineage. The members of the dominant lineage may indeed be in a minority. There is, in other words, a link between lineages and tribal segments, often the tribal segment being known by the same name as the lineage.

The clan as a whole is dispersed. This means that when there is a quarrel the kin, who by custom support one another on the one side, may be mixed up with the kin of the other side, and such a quarrel may well provoke a direct threat to the unity of a territorial community. This can be seen, to put it mildly, to be a most tiresome eventuality, and clearly kinsmen are likely to try to pour oil on troubled waters rather than have their local day-to-day relationships frequently and violently upset. Men will be persuaded to settle their disputes quickly and without fuss.

Even though the situation is structured in such a way as to lead to pressure being put on people to compose their differences, some quarrels are bound to develop into bitter strife. How, then, is order maintained? In answering this, Evans-Pritchard paradoxically points to the institution of the feud.

If one man kills another he will go immediately to a person known as a leopard-skin chief. He is a man who wears a leopard skin, but he is in no sense a chief but rather a person who performs certain ritual acts. The murderer will give him a beast to sacrifice, and then will submit to having his arm cut so that the blood flows—this symbolises the getting rid of the murdered man's blood. As long as the murderer stays with the leopard-skin chief he is in sanctuary. Meanwhile, the kin of the dead man seek vengeance, but are unable to achieve it. A few weeks are allowed to pass during which tempers may cool a little. Then the leopard-skin chief will approach the murdered man's kin to see what compensation they will accept, having previously seen what is likely to be offered. He will strongly urge that compensation be accepted, threatening to curse them if they do not; a device that enables them to save face. Custom supports the necessity for compromise, meanwhile restrictions are imposed on both parties who may not eat or drink from the same vessels or eat in the home of a third person together. Thus, if members of opposing kin are domiciled closely the restrictions may be an irritant assisting in promoting a quick settlement. Eventually cattle will be offered and accepted as compensation, and sacrifices and ritual cleansing bring the affair to a close; at least for a time.

It should be noted that the leopard-skin chief is neither a negotiator nor a judge, but merely a go-between; he has no power except the sacredness of his person. Clearly, settlements are more easily reached between members of tertiary segments than secondary ones, whilst a feud between tribes may never be settled; but then it is difficult to organise a tribal feud, the spatial distances being a mitigating factor.

We are concerned here with a society which has no law and which can hardly be said to have political institutions. Yet there is a system that maintains order. It is difficult to point very clearly to it in terms of functionally related social institutions. In rather technical terms, Evans-Pritchard sums up the situation when he says: "The process consists of complementary tendencies towards fission and fusion which, operating alike in all political groups by a series of inclusions and exclusions that are controlled by the changing social situation, enable us to speak of a system and to say that this system is characteristically defined by the relativity and opposition of its segments" [1940(b), p. 296]. Or, as Gluckman has neatly put it, there is "peace in the feud" [1955(b)]. Not that feuds never happen, but that out of the very conflicts themselves loyalties are born, for a man is pulled into relationships with different people as allies or enemies according to the situation.

Contrasted Political Systems

Briefly, and we fear inadequately, we have outlined two contrasting political systems; one displaying well-developed legal organisation, the other having no law in the strict sense of the term. Fortes and Evans-Pritchard, in their comparative study of African societies, point to two main types of political system, of which these may be regarded as examples, but they present others [1940(b)], and quite recently more have been described (Middleton and Tait, 1958). Thus we may, for instance, group together the Zulu, the BaMangwato, the BaBemba, the BaNyankole, and the small Nigerian people known as the Kede. All these, on the one hand, illustrate societies having strong centralised authorities with administrative machinery and constituted legal institutions. On the other hand, there are, in addition to the Nuer, the Logoli and the Tallensi who lack these things. Size of country and population does not seem to be relevant to the distinction, but these writers suggest that those societies which are culturally heterogenous tend to develop a state-like structure, and that marked differences in culture and economic pursuits are incompatible with segmentary structures of the second type.

What we may say also is that in all societies there are conflicts and that a social system must contain them. In the centralised type of society we may discern all kinds of checks and balances; the Swazi offer many illustrations of these, but so also do the Barotse and the Zulu. Conflicts are clearly seen among the Nuer, but they are of a different kind and are contained in a different way. In the one case they are institutionalised in councils or courts, or different institutions reinforce but also check the exercise of power. Both rights and duties inhere in kingship, counselling, and citizenship; such rights and duties are common knowledge; they are upheld by common values. In the other case there is equilibrium between the segments of the social structure, for stability follows from the total interaction of segmented relationships.

What we are saying is that there is more than one way in which societies may arrange their affairs so that order is maintained

internally and their existence ensured in the wider environment.
And also that certain recognisable types of political systems may be
discerned. It is in the classification and comparison of such types
that we may be led to fuller understanding of political systems, their
constituents, and the interrelationships of these constituent elements.

BIBLIOGRAPHY AND FURTHER READING

Evans-Pritchard, E. E., *The Nuer: A Description of the Modes
    of Livelihood and Political Institutions of a Nilotic People*,
    1940(a) (Clarendon Press).
    Kinship and Marriage among the Nuer, 1951 (Clarendon Press).
Evans-Pritchard, E. E., and Fortes, M., Eds., *African Political
    Systems*, 1940(b) (O.U.P. for the International African
    Institute).
Gluckman, Max. "The Lozi of Barotseland in North-Western Rho-
    desia", *Seven Tribes of British Central Africa*, Eds. E.
    Colson and M. Gluckman, 1951 (O.U.P.).
    The Judicial Process among the Barotse of Northern Rhodesia,
    1955(a) (Manchester Univ. Press).
    Custom and Conflict in Africa, 1955(b) (Blackwell).
    Politics, Law and Ritual in Tribal Society, 1965 (Blackwell).
Homans, G. C., *The Human Group*, 1951 (Routledge and Kegan
    Paul).
Klein, J., *The Study of Groups*, 1956 (Routledge and Kegan Paul).
Kuper, H., *An African Aristocracy: Rank among the Swazi of the
    Protectorate*, 1947 (O.U.P.).
Malinowski, B., *Crime and Custom in Savage Society*, 1926
    (Harcourt).
Middleton, J., and Tait, D., Eds., *Tribes Without Rulers*, 1958
    (Routledge and Kegan Paul).
Radcliffe-Brown, A. R., "Primitive Law", *Encyclopaedia of the
    Social Sciences*, 1933. Reprinted in his *Structure and Func-
    tion in Primitive Society*, 1952.

CHAPTER VI

SYSTEMS OF BELIEFS AND RITUAL

Primitive Mentality

It is useful to begin a discussion of beliefs and ritual practices by considering the mentality of simple peoples. It is useful to do so because perhaps nowhere has more prejudice been expressed or misunderstanding displayed than on this subject. The early missionaries who set out in the wake of the explorers and traders did so with the intention of converting the heathen to their own views: religious, moral, and social. This in itself may well be regarded as reasonable from their point of view, but it must be said of many of them that in setting about their task they assumed that "primitive" beliefs were *necessarily* inferior to their own, and they made this assumption because they also assumed that "primitive" thought was necessarily inferior. For this untested assumption they were partly, but not entirely, responsible. Early sociologists and anthropologists, preoccupied with the evolutionary hypothesis, had assumed that the simple societies were relics of primitive times, and concluded that their thought must be inferior to that of the more advanced peoples with whom they identified themselves. The result was that few investigations were made into the nature of the beliefs and the practices we are concerned with, although one notable exception among the missionaries was Bishop Codrington.

Nevertheless, curiosity about the strange and esoteric led to the collection of information, but scholars who undertook this work usually cast their explanations in an evolutionary scheme of thought. A notable example is the monumental work of Sir James Frazer, whose *Golden Bough* was first published in 1890 and extended to twelve volumes by 1915. Yet although gradually an immense amount of information was assembled little of it was systematically related to other aspects of the societies to which it was relevant. Moreover, prejudice lingers, and even to-day there are widespread

misconceptions about the rationality and intelligence of the kinds
of people we are interested in.

Even so eminent and able a scholar as L. Lévy-Bruhl has been
impressed by the irrationality of the "primitive mentality", holding
that it could be characterised as "pre-logical", that their cultural
heritage was such that members of these societies were conditioned
from childhood in a manner that prevented them from fully appreciating natural causation (1925). Now whilst there is some evidence
partially supporting this view there is also much to support a very
different view, namely, that over wide areas of social life all peoples
act reasonably, that they think in terms of what we call natural
causation, and that they are able to plan to use the means at their
disposal for the achievement of ends.

Moreover, there is perhaps a danger on our part that by contrast we fail to appreciate the irrationalities in our own behaviour
in our society. Generally, we may say that given certain assumptions—and all thought starts from assumptions—all men display in
varying degrees the ability to reason, but that the assumptions may
be vastly different. Thus we shall later endeavour to show that
witchcraft, for instance, whilst it may strike us as thoroughly
irrational may yet show a high degree of rational consistency, given
the particular assumptions that those who believe in the power of
witchcraft do in fact make. Evidence pointing to the oddness of
simple societies must not blind us to what is common and familiar,
for whilst a people may practise magic and witchcraft they do
possess also a knowledge of the natural world in which they live,
for otherwise they would have no technology and economy whereby
to live.

It was much of the burden of a celebrated essay by Malinowski
(1925) to point out that the Melanesian peoples he studied in the
Trobriand Archipelago are industrious traders, fishermen, and,
above all, agriculturalists of no mean ability and possessing a knowledge of the techniques required to produce even more food than
they need. Partly their success is due to the favourable soil and
climate, but chiefly he attributed it to their extensive knowledge of
types of soil and the crops suitable to be grown on them, an appreciation of the value of an orderly cycle of operations determined by
the seasons and the weather, and the good sense to work hard and

accurately. They know about insect pests and all the other hazards to growing crops, and they do their best to ensure the success of their work. All this depends on their knowledge of natural conditions and on applying their knowledge in a rational and orderly manner. Yet they use magic.

Magical rites are performed over their gardens in a regular sequence; in fact, the leadership of their agricultural enterprise is in the hands of the magicians. It might seem at first sight as if the rational and the irrational activities are mixed up and the Melanesians unable to distinguish between their effects. If an inhabitant of these Pacific islands were to be asked why he uses magic, doubtless he would reply that not to do so would render his gardens liable to attack by blight, bush-pigs, or locusts, or that his work would be destroyed by drought or flood. Bad work, he well knows, will reap its own poor reward. Yet even when he has done his best and taken every precaution and applied all his knowledge of techniques to the task there is always the possibility that some disaster may overtake his labours, a disaster following from events over which he has no control in terms of his technical knowledge. For these occasions he requires magic as a safeguard. Moreover, the man who leads the work in the gardens performs two quite distinct functions, says Malinowski, and people are conscious of his twofold role. He is the leader of the workers and he is also the magician; the two roles are separate but complementary.

This distinction between magic and technology may be seen in other activities. Thus Malinowski points to the not uncomplicated techniques for rigging out dug-out canoes for open-sea fishing; canoes which must be well constructed and manned by experienced men for the hazardous fishing operations they undertake. Yet again, with all the detailed knowledge they possess, such fishing trips are liable to encounter strong and incalculable tides, monsoon gales, and unknown reefs. Hence magic is also practised during the building of the canoe and before open-sea fishing takes place. It is interesting to note that where fishing in inner lagoons is carried on, and fish are poisoned and catches obtained without any hazards at all, the people do not practise magic.

This observation led Malinowski to consider a psychological explanation of magical practices, for he held that it is under conditions of uncertainty and risk, where there is danger and insecurity, that recourse is had to this means. It is, in other words, a means for coping with emotional stress.

Again, it seems that the natural causes leading to sickness and death are appreciated by these people, yet when a particular man is sick he is apt to attribute his fate to sorcery rather than to natural causes, but not so others who are spectators of his ill-health. The fact is that the two causal factors are often held to obtain at the same time. A man may suffer and see his sufferings as a result of natural causes, but also seek to explain them in terms of supernatural causation. This is particularly so, as we shall see, in the phenomenon of witchcraft.

Witchcraft in Zandeland

Perhaps the best study of witchcraft, certainly of witchcraft in Africa, is that made by Evans-Pritchard (1937). His account is of the Azande, a people living in the Nile-Congo divide. They are a people with a royal aristocracy which is proud and conservative, and authoritarianism in both the family and the society generally is very noticeable. They are agriculturalists, growing eleusine, maize, sweet potatoes, manioc, groundnuts, and other plants; they hunt and fish; and they are skilled craftsmen in pottery, wood carving, and basket-work. They are a friendly and intelligent people, willing to learn and to accept innovations from others, and they sensibly concern themselves for the most part with the normal daily round of mundane activities in circumstances of reasonable security and well-being.

The Azande, however, believe that some people are witches who are able to injure them as a consequence of some inherent quality. A witch, according to them, is distinguished from a sorcerer, for the former does not perform a magic rite or utter a spell and he uses no medicines, whilst the latter may use bad medicine and practise a rite to harm someone. To counter witchcraft and sorcery the Azande use diviners and medicine, and they appeal to oracles. They believe that witchcraft is a substance in the abdomen and that it is inherited from parent to child; the sons of a male witch are witches but not his daughters, although the latter may inherit witchcraft from their mother if she is a witch. Although it would follow that if a man was a witch his entire male kin would also be witches the Azande, in practice, only regard close paternal kinsmen as witches. If a man is found to be a witch his clan may deny his biological relationship to them; they may say he is a bastard.

The Azande, like many other people, are fully aware that there are natural explanations for natural phenomena, but where human health and well-being are adversely affected they want an additional explanation. If a man goes out into the bush and is trampled to death by an elephant his kin ask why he was killed. They are well aware that he died as a result of multiple injuries which resulted in his bodily organisms being irreparably damaged, but they also ask why *this* man was killed by *this* elephant at *this* particular time and in *this* particular place, and not another man by another means at another time and place, and the answer they give is that the man was bewitched. Someone with evil intent was responsible for so influencing the course of events that they led to the man's death. Or a man may fall ill from food poisoning. The Azande understand this, but witchcraft answers the question why this man fell ill when others did not. Thus for every misfortune there is the question "how?" and the question "why?" it occurred, and the second question is always answered in terms of witchcraft. It follows that social justice demands that the guilty person be detected and taken to task for his actions; death, in particular, must be avenged.

Any misfortune may be attributed to witchcraft: a man may lose the affection of his wife, his crops may fail, his child may injure itself, or it may be some quite minor matter, but all the same he will attribute them to the same cause; indeed, sometimes a man experiencing some small discomfort or being somewhat put out by an unexpected occurrence will say "it's witchcraft", much as we should say "just my luck". Witchcraft, then, is pervasive in the society, but it arouses no undue sense of eeriness or fear, and appears to be commonplace; something to be regarded for the most part in a matter-of-fact manner.

Witchcraft does not cause a man to do wrong, or tell lies, for the Azande hold a man responsible for his actions, but the person who suffers for another's wrong may ask himself why this happened to him, why his wife committed adultery and not some other man's, why his crops were stolen rather than his neighbours, and witchcraft will account for it.

The Use of Oracles and Diviners

There are various means employed for detecting witches, among them being oracles. One of these is the rubbing-board oracle. This consists of a small circular wooden platform of few inches in diameter having two short legs at one end and a tail-piece; it is laid to rest on the ground and another small circular platform or lid with a small knob on top fits on to this circular base. The base is treated with juices of various plants and then addressed by the enquirer. He will put a question, the answer to which may be given in a simple affirmative or denial. Accordingly, as to whether the lid when grasped sticks or runs smoothly over the base part, so he has his answer.

A second is the termite oracle. Two sticks of different trees are placed in a termite mound. A question is put to the oracle and next day the sticks are examined to see which one the ants have eaten. It is held to be more reliable than the rubbing-board oracle, for the latter may possibly be misused and a man may cheat by making it stick, but the termite oracle has its own disadvantages, for only one question can be put at a time and it takes a day before the answer can be obtained.

Most reliable of all is the poison oracle, which is used by other people in Africa besides the Azande. A poison having a strychnine content is obtained from a forest creeper and made into a paste. Some of the liquid is squeezed out of the paste into a chicken's beak, as a result of which it either vomits or dies; the amount of the poison administered seems to have no connection with its fate. Although a chicken may go into a spasm and die, as often it survives. According to whether it dies or lives so the enquirer has his answer. If a man is anxious about his affairs he will address the oracle in some such fashion as: "Poison oracle, poison oracle, will Zakiri fall sick if he goes to Nuerland. Zakiri will fall sick poison oracle kill the fowl, Zakiri will not fall sick poison oracle spare the fowl". Having obtained his reply he may want to check it, in which case he puts the question differently. If the fowl died he will say, "Poison oracle has declared Zakiri will fall sick if he goes to Nuerland. If the declaration is true poison oracle spare the fowl, if it is false poison oracle kill the fowl". If the fowl lives then it is confirmed, but if the second fowl dies the answer is unconfirmed and the test invalidated for this question; but a man will try again, time and chickens permitting, and an Azande, we are told, will always find time.

Besides using oracles an Azande will consult diviners, but these have a reliability about as good or bad as the rubbing-board oracle. They constitute a means for carrying out preliminary investigations, reducing the number of suspected witches to a few; then it is that the termite or, better still, the poison oracle is consulted. It is important at this stage to point to the distinction between witchcraft and magic, for the witch does harm unwittingly, whereas magic is deliberate, and if evil is intended it is sorcery, but, of course, there is good magic. However, magic is defined as good or bad according to moral ideas. Thus a man may practise good magic to injure a recalcitrant witch; but, then, this is only justice. If a man injures the person or goods of another he is taken to court, but if he is injured by someone unknown recourse is had to magic. Through witch-doctors and oracles a man may detect his enemy; he will then throw down a chicken wing before his door. Compensation may be obtained and a promise made to refrain from bewitching him. If the matter is serious it will be decided by the courts, the prince's oracle being the final determinant of guilt.

Scepticism, Faith, Morals, and Politics

Now there are a number of interesting features in this example. One is the fact that despite a certain degree of scepticism, both about a man's claim to being bewitched and about the claims of witch-doctors, Azande have a firm faith in magic and particularly in witchcraft. No amount of argument will shake their faith, and the reason is not far to seek, for theirs is a closed system of thought. Assuming the validity of a belief in witches they can always divine who is bewitching a man; he in turn is unconscious of his errors; to prove he is innocent he appeals to oracles, but successful or not he thereby affirms his belief in the power of oracles and the existence of witchcraft. If an oracle fails then that, too, is attributed to witchcraft. Nowhere can one break into this closed circle. Even if a witch-doctor is discovered cheating or is unable to divine or solve a puzzle, the prior belief in magic powers leads people to comment on the better witch-doctors who live elsewhere. As Evans-Pritchard argues, witchcraft, oracles, and magic all combine and are all interrelated in such a way as to preserve the system of beliefs and maintain faith in the rites performed. Thus death is held to be a proof of witchcraft which is avenged by means of magic, but the achievement of vengeance through magic is proved by the poison oracle, and the accuracy of the latter is determined by the king's oracle, which no one doubts. If magic fails it fails only in the instance, for the Azande do not generalise its failure to all magic. The scepticism that they display is specific; it is scepticism regarding a particular magical rite, a specific medicine or individual witch-doctor, which by contrast establishes the general rule that others are sound.

Yet another point to be noted is that when a man seeks to know who is bewitching him his attention is directed towards his enemies, for this system of beliefs is related to morality. Only a witch who hates a man will bewitch him. Clearly, to keep out of trouble one must be on good terms with one's neighbour, be kind and courteous, respect his property and his wife. Only a witch with vicious attitudes and feelings will harm people.

Speaking generally of this phenomenon, Gluckman argues that witchcraft as a theory of causation embraces a theory of morals, for witches are immoral when they bewitch someone (1955). They may be good members of the community and still be witches, but then their witchcraft is "cool" or inactive. Of course, people who accuse others of witchcraft may also be immoral, for their accusations may spring from envy or jealousy. This is well known, and many accusations are discounted in the light of what people know of the characters and circumstances of the accuser.

Witchcraft is bound up with social relationships. The fact that among the Azande it is inherited in the agnatic line, unusual for Africa, where elsewhere it descends from women to their children, may be of some significance. For the Azande believe it to be impossible for a man to bewitch a near paternal relative, and particularly for a man and his son to bewitch each other. A psychologist may argue that this permits filial resentment against authoritarian parental control to be diverted outside the agnatic group, thus providing an integrating mechanism for the family whose members come together in a common aim of seeking vengeance. This, in fact, seems to be what Gluckman is suggesting when he says that "we shall not be able to understand the sociology of Azande witchcraft, as against its intellectual logic, until we understand the significance of the vengeance group in Azande society" (*ibid.*, p. 91). For witchcraft does not seem to be just hostility and hatred displayed in an unusual form, but rather the exhibition of hatred in some social relationships and not in others.

There is, moreover, not merely a connection between witchcraft and kinship, but between witchcraft and the legal and political systems. Thus the fact that witch-doctors form a kind of professional corporation advising clients, advocating and defending their interests with appeal to oracles for confirmation or denial of accusations, points to their quasi-legal standing. That the ultimate oracular appeal is to the king's oracle means that power to control the system lies in the hands of the central authority. It can thus be seen that witchcraft as a system of beliefs and practices is self-maintaining, in this society at least, and it may be shown to be so in others; it is related to other social institutions, particularly kinship and political institutions.

There are an enormous number and variety of ritual practices in simple societies. Some are quite obviously related to the political system, as, for instance, the rites connected with the annual "drama of kingship" ceremonies recounted of the Swazi by H. Kuper (1947), where the rites performed reinforce the unity of the nation, but also, as Gluckman points out, affirm all the conflicts that centre around the person of the reigning king (*op. cit.*, p. 123). Some rites relate to the economy and to the land and its fertility, and these we have touched on earlier. Yet others concern what are known as *rites de passage*, that is to say, the ritual of socially distinguished phases in the life history of an individual. Thus initiation rites are practised in most simple societies, their content bearing reference to the adult male and female position or status of the initiated and the new responsibilities they assume in society. Frequently these rites involve an endurance trial or some painful experiences, physical, emotional, or both, and often the initiated is marked on his body, if a male by circumcision or sub-incision, or, perhaps, by having a tooth knocked out as a sign of his new position in the community.

Religion and Magic

Thus far we have spoken of beliefs and rites; in doing so we have distinguished magic and witchcraft, and we have shown that sorcery is different from both although it involves magic and has some resemblance to witchcraft. We have said nothing specifically as yet about religion. How is religion to be distinguished from these other beliefs and ritual practices?

In the first place, we may point to the social character of religion. It is something shared by a community and participated in by groups of people, if not by the entire community then by a section of it, perhaps consisting only of a group of kinsmen. Magic, more often than not, and certainly black magic, is a private affair.

Moreover, religion is always approved of, whereas magic may be harmful and so opposed by the community. Both seem to be concerned with a supernatural world, but whereas magic seeks to alter circumstances and environment religion is more concerned with the subjective state of the believer; frequently it is the case that religion is the means whereby a person seeks to make an adjustment, to change his attitudes and affections, indeed, to know how he shall act. There is, in other words, a manipulative element in magic that is not strictly paralleled in religion.

To be sure, a man may sacrifice to a deity or pray that circumstances may alter, but no automatic mechanical response is expected as it is in magic, for the deity having personal qualities is not fully known and may act differently to the way desired. Magic may be regarded, perhaps, as a kind of supernatural technology where the practitioner is required to have a certain kind of knowledge or ability, possession of which enables him to achieve ends in the natural world by unnatural means.

The similarities of the two seem to lie in the fact that they are both concerned with a supernatural dimension and they both involve beliefs and rites. Inability to appreciate in religion the profundity of beliefs and the intricacies of symbolism in rites has led to a too facile comparison with magic. Whilst distinguishing the two phenomena many writers appear to regard them as closely related. Thus Davis says that religion represents one pole of a range of phenomena which at the other pole shades into magic. "Thus we should not think of the difference between magic and religion as a rigid dichotomy," he says, "but rather as a wide gradation involving several rather independent variables" (1948, p. 537). This is a view also held by Goode (1951). Both writers see a similarity in terms of the supernatural reference of both phenomena. The same view has been held by others, notably by Malinowski who offered much the same kind of psychological explanation for them (*op. cit.*).

There is, however, a marked difference between the two, setting them quite apart. Magic is always concerned with practical mundane matters, whereas religion more often is concerned with ultimates: a man's relation to his god or gods, to his ancestral spirits, to his totem. When we describe such phenomena, which we term religious, we are, in fact, describing those beliefs and ritual activities that a person is concerned with when he is most aware of his very existence. Religion is mostly important to mankind at times of personal crisis or when new and socially significant stages of the life-cycle are approached: at birth, initiation, marriage, death; although it is not restricted to these. Religion is at once a private and a communal matter, and yet the private aspect is related to the social and vice versa. Among the simple peoples the communal aspect of religion stands out clearly. It is largely because of this that modern social anthropologists, eschewing historical explanations, have sought to discern the social function of religion. They have not been unsuccessful.

Before, however, we indicate the lines along which they have thought about this subject, let us note one significant feature of religious behaviour. This is the attitude that is frequently found to be adopted by men at worship or in taking part in ritual activities of a religious nature. Attitudes of reverence, awe, despair, or exultation are usually discerned. There is little of the matter-of-factness which so many observers of magic have noted. The distinction is related to that between the sacred and the profane. It is difficult to see a sacred element in magic, although it is concerned with the supernatural, but the sacred element in religion is most noticeable. The awe and reverence of the religious devotee is directed to the sacred or the holy.

The Social Function of Religion

Without endeavouring to explain religion in its entirety, or commenting on the truth or falsity of beliefs or the effectiveness or ineffectiveness of rites, which is not the proper task of the sociologist, we may indicate its social function. But to do this we need not, following Durkheim, rashly identify the sacred with society (1926). It must be said, however, that Durkheim's work has led to an advance in our understanding of the relationship of the individual to his group; it has pointed to the way in which social solidarity is enhanced as a result of ritual activities by members of a group, be that group a family worshipping at an ancestral shrine or a tribal group like the Murngin of Australia ceremonially eating their totem.

The fact is that man is both a natural and a spiritual being, and it is from this conjunction that religion is born. Thus he is concerned about his relationship to nature, time, and his fellows, and to the superempirical realm to which these are related. That he is a member of society means that at some points and to some degree religion is a social matter; and for this reason it is an essential subject for sociological investigation.

In the life-cycle, as we have pointed out, religion is related to significant changes in a man's position in society, and we find universally religious practices connected with these changes. Apart from these occasions there are others which more closely relate to the existence, identity, and well-being of his society, whence we see national religious events and systems of beliefs corresponding to them. These vary greatly according to the structure of the society. They differ according to the kind of economy, whence we see differential emphasis placed, say, on fertility rites; or according to the kind of political system, whence we see differential emphasis placed, say, on kingship; or according to the kind of family structure, whence we see differential emphasis placed, say, on family gods or ancestral spirits. Doubtless, it is partly because of the wide variations in social structures that there is such a rich variation in religious beliefs and practices.

As yet, sociologists have hardly begun to analyse and compare religious systems of simple societies, despite the vast collection of data at their disposal. Although it should be said that the sociological analysis of religions in relation to social structure has strikingly been done with regard to some of the high religions (of Europe, India, China, and Ancient Judaism) by Max Weber (1925-7), as it has by Fustel de Coulanges with regard to the ancient religions of Greece and Rome in a classic work entitled *La Cité antique*, published in 1864.

One of the clearest formulations of the hypothesis of the social function of religion was made by Radcliffe-Brown in his work on the Andamanese (1922) and restated in his essay on "Religion and Society" (1952, Chap. VIII), where he says: "Stated in the simplest possible terms the theory is that an orderly social life amongst human beings depends upon the presence in the minds of members of a society of certain sentiments, which control the behaviour of the individual in his relation to others. Rites can be seen to be the regulated symbolic expressions of certain sentiments. Rites can therefore be shown to have a specific social function when, and to the extent that, they have for their effect to regulate, maintain, and transmit from one generation to another sentiments on which the constitution of the society depends" (p. 157). Taking two different types of religion, ancestor worship in ancient China and Australian totemism, he shows how in both it is possible to demonstrate the close correspondence of the form of the religion and the form of social structure, and how in each case the religion contributes to the social cohesion of the society.

Similar comparative studies have been carried out by Goode, who discusses the relation of religion to economy, politics, and kinship in five simple societies each widely separated from the others, namely the Dahomey, the Manus, the Tikopia, the Zuni Pueblo Indians, and the Murngin (1951). This kind of study has a close relationship to the tradition referred to in Chapter I known as the *sociology of knowledge*, for in the case of religious beliefs, as in the case of moral, intellectual, and political ideas, we can by means of a sociological analysis discern their relationship to the structure of human society. As we saw in Chapter II, the structure of social positions is related to the norms of a society in terms of role-playing. However, a well-developed system of beliefs or ideas may possess a developing life of its own. It may thus give rise to social innovations, sometimes of far-reaching importance.

As far as the present study of simple societies is concerned, social anthropologists are aware that to shed light on such phenomena as taboos, totemic observances, and ritual uncleanness more detailed analyses and further comparative studies will have to be carried out. The stage which has been reached so far is that of obtaining accurate ethnological descriptions, such as those sponsored by the International African Institute, of religious beliefs and practices (1954).

BIBLIOGRAPHY AND FURTHER READING

Davis, K., *Human Society*, 1948 (Macmillan, New York).

Durkheim, Emile, *The Elementary Forms of Religious Life*, 1915, *trans.* 1954 (Allen and Unwin).

Evans-Pritchard, E. E., *Witchcraft Oracles and Magic among the Azande*, 1937 (Clarendon Press).

Gluckman, Max, *Custom and Conflict in Africa*, 1955 (Blackwell).

Goode, W. J., *Religion among the Primitives*, 1951 (Free Press).

International African Institute, *African Worlds: Studies in the Cosmological Ideas and Social Values of African Peoples*, 1954.

Kuper, H., *An African Aristocracy: Rank among the Swazi of the Protectorate*, 1947 (O.U.P.).

Lévy-Bruhl, L. *Primitive Mentality*, 1923 (Macmillan and Co.).

Malinowski, B., "Magic, Science, and Religion", *Science, Religion, and Reality*, Ed. J. Needham, 1925. Reprinted in *Magic, Science, and Religion, and other Essays*, 1948 (Free Press).

Radcliffe-Brown, A. R., *The Andaman Islanders*, 1922 (Macmillan and Co.).

Structure and Function in Primitive Society, 1952 (Cohen and West).

Robertson, R. (Edit.), *Sociology of Religion: Selected Readings*, 1969 (Penguin).

Weber, Max., *Gesammelte Aufsätze zur Religionssoziologie*, 3 vols., 1925-7. Translated *The Protestant Ethic and the Spirit of Capitalism*, 1930 (Scribner). *The Religion of China*, 1951 (Free Press). *Ancient Judaism*, 1952 (Free Press). *The Sociology of Religion*, 1965 (Methuen). Other portions in *From Max Weber: Essays in Sociology*, Eds. H. Gerth and C. W. Mills, 1947 (Routledge and Kegan Paul).

PART III
SYSTEMATIC ANALYSIS OF THE COMPLEX SOCIETY

CHAPTER VII

THE SYSTEM OF SOCIAL STRATIFICATION

The Complex Society

Turning from the simple to the complex society, and having in mind chiefly America and Britain, we find that kinship, which loomed so large in our discussion of the simple society, now recedes into the background; its place is taken by the system of stratification. It is not that kinship in the complex society is altogether unimportant, nor that stratification is absent in the simple society, but in the latter it is often less integral to social organisation than kinship and in the former it is pervasive throughout. Indeed, whatever the aspect of urban industrial society we are studying stratification must also be considered, for the complex society is highly differentiated. This, Adam Smith noted, was the most significant feature of the emerging industrial society of Britain in the late eighteenth century, for he opened his discussion in *An Inquiry into the Nature and Causes of the Wealth of Nations* (1776) with a lengthy description of the division of labour underlying the developing economy.

In an elaborate and highly developed economy there are, of course, a very large number of social positions, but differentiation is found elsewhere as well as in the economy; it is found in administration, government, and education, in the specialised medical and social services, in recreation and entertainment, and so forth. Complementary to this division of labour with its differentiation of social positions, there is differentiation in outlook and in experience, in interest and in knowledge, in mode of living and in aspiration.

Now what is differentiated is also evaluated. Thus it comes about that whilst social positions are differently valued, there is broad but by no means complete agreement of evaluations. We shall have to ask to what extent there is a clear ranking of social positions, to what extent there is agreement about such ranking, and to what extent this stratification or ranking affects the process of social life. Firstly, let us examine briefly some of the more prominent kinds of analyses of this phenomenon of social stratification.

The Marxian Analysis

Marx, as we saw in Chapter I, held that history was the story of class struggles. The stratification of society he saw as an age-old phenomenon. In the Roman Empire there was a clearly discernible division of patricians and plebeians. In Medieval times society was divided into *estates*; these formed a broadly-based pyramid with the king at the apex, a ranking which in France, for example, had crystallised into the three estates of clergy, nobles, and "commoners" long before the time of the Revolution. In his own day Marx perceived Europe as divided into class-structured societies; various strata could be detected, but the process of social change, he believed, was leading to the formation of only two, the great antagonistic classes of Bourgeoisie and Proletariat.

Marx did not examine very closely the differences between classes and estates, nor did he have anything to say about *castes*, which still exist in India and Ceylon. Present-day sociologists do distinguish between these various kinds of stratification. Moreover, there is to-day a more analytical approach to the subject, so that distinctions are made also between generally desired social values such as wealth, prestige, and power. Marx would have argued that these usually go together and that the distinctions between them are unimportant. For Marx the important feature of our kind of society was the source of these values, and this, he thought, lay in a person's relationship to the means of production; in other words, in the economy.

In the European countries of Marx's time with their capitalistic type of economy the social strata were in conflict with each other; the revolutions of 1848 emphasised this fact. He saw that these conflicts were concerned with the distribution of wealth between classes; he noted growing class consciousness resulting from the better communications linking people together and from better education; he was aware of the growing dissatisfaction on the part of the Proletariat at being excluded from participation in the control of the economy and thus leading to the development of their organisation politically.

What is important in an estimate of Marx's thought is that he pointed, on the one hand, to certain objective features of stratification, aggregates of people classed in terms of their relationships to the economy, and on the other hand to the subjective element of

class consciousness, a consciousness that would develop as industrialisation proceeded. It should be observed, however, that Marx
believed that this element of class consciousness was exacerbated
by, if not rooted in, the class antagonism he sought to detect in all
types of society and to be especially obvious in the overt behaviour
of members of capitalist societies. Although his ideas on this subject have in the event been discredited, but not perhaps so largely as
has sometimes been suggested (as will emerge in later references to
modern sociological investigations), it remains true that Marx's
emphasis on both the relationship of class to the economy, and the
importance of class consciousness in social stratification, was to
influence many subsequent sociologists, even though some laid more
emphasis on one aspect than another.

Weber's Analytical Distinctions

One of the sociologists influenced by Marx was Max Weber,
who, whilst he was not at all satisfied with the Marxian thesis,
endeavoured, like him, to carry out a thorough-going analysis of
the socio-economic system known as Capitalism. In the process of
doing this Weber has left us with a brief but incisive discussion
of social stratification. The relevant section of his *Wirtschaft und
Gesellschaft* has been translated and published as an essay entitled
"Class, Status, and Party" [1947(*a*)], and there is another short
chapter included in *The Theory of Social and Economic Organisation* [1947(*b*)] from the same work. His very important contribution to our understanding of social stratification centres in his
distinction between *class* and *status*.

What does he mean by "class"? The first thing to notice is that
he does not regard classes as communities or social groups; nevertheless, classes may and frequently do provide the bases for con-
certed action. Classes are defined in terms of opportunities, or, as
he calls them, "life-chances". Where an aggregate of people have
similar social opportunities, and where these opportunities depend
on their possessions or facilities for acquiring the necessary income,
both possessions and facilities being relevant to a market economy,
then there we have a class situation, and the people constitute a
class.

This definition is an economic one, people being classed according to their relationship to property and source of income. The

fundamental distinction between classes is, of course, that between those who have property and the propertyless, but there are other distinctions to be made among those who have property; chief of these is the distinction between *rentiers*, whose income is derived from share dividends, rents, interest on bonds, and so forth, and *entrepreneurs*, who control the use of economic resources, money, credit, and so forth. Again, those who have no property may be differentiated according to the kinds of skills and services they offer on the market. There is, for example, a distinction to be made between the skilled and the unskilled manual worker, and yet another between both of these classes and the professional classes. There is, says Weber, a conflict between classes, for the economy is a competitive one, and to varying degrees these classes are all involved in a struggle with each other—a struggle which extends beyond the bounds of the economy and into the political system.

Status groups, unlike classes, are communities, or at least there is interaction between the members. They are groups where the members consider each other to be equals, and where they also evaluate their group relative to other groups in terms of prestige or, as Weber says, "honour".

There is a link between class and status, for members of the same status group frequently stand in the same class relationship to each other. But the common class position does not provide a qualification for status, it does not automatically confer prestige; indeed, propertied and propertyless may belong to the same status group. The significant feature of a status group is that its members share a certain manner of life distinguishable from that of other status groups. It may be observed of two status groups that if the mode of life, or "style of life" as Weber described it, distinguishing them alters so that the distinction becomes difficult to discern, then novel features will be introduced to restore the distinction; here is one source of fashion.

Members of a status group share certain conventions and acknowledge certain symbols of their status; their most pronounced feature is a tendency to endogamy. They maintain their distinctiveness by convention and custom, but sometimes these may harden into law, as, for example, when sumptuary laws set down what is considered to be appropriate clothing for different groups; and when this kind of event takes place we have what are called *estates*, that is to say, status groups where status differences are maintained in law.

One status group may be distinguished in very rigid terms from another, particularly if the members of each are of different ethnic composition; in such cases the status groups usually become *castes*. Neither estates nor castes concern us in a descriptive analysis of the social systems of America and Britain to-day, although sometimes superficial similarities have tempted sociologists to discuss the relationships of white to negro in America, especially in the Southern States, in terms of caste.

Weber makes a general distinction when he says that classes are stratified according to their relationships to the production and acquisition of wealth, whereas status groups are stratified according to the patterns of consumption of wealth, for a mode or style of life is definable in terms of consumption patterns: type of dwelling and neighbourhood, food habits, kind of education, recreational activities, and so forth. If status distinctions harden into legal distinctions at one extreme, it must not be forgotten that at the other extreme, that is in their origin, they arise from usurpation.

Moreover, since the abolition of legal differences in our society, and the development of what T. H. Marshall (1950) calls the concept of citizenship, there is greater scope for pretence to status. The pretentions of status groups and the nature of invidious distinctions is generally an entertaining subject, as has recently been shown by both Pear (1955) and Mitford (1955), and more quantitatively by Chapman (1955). Those that obtained in America at the close of the nineteenth century have been analysed in a famous book by Thorstein Veblen, which is amusing despite its pedantry and no less so for the seriousness with which it was written (1899).

A status group endeavours to make distinctions of social worth without reference to wealth. Hence the acquisition of wealth is no sure means whereby to obtain acceptance by a status group. As Weber points out, and as countless novelists have too, the *nouveaux riches* are never fully assimilated to a status group higher in the system than they were born to, although their children may be.

What, then, is the relationship of class to status? Weber points to two different conditions of the socio-economic structure of society. "When the bases of the acquisition and distribution of

soc.   8 goods are relatively stable, stratification by status is favoured. Every technological repercussion and economic transformation threatens stratification by status and pushes the class situation into the foreground. Epochs and countries in which the naked class situation is of predominant significance are regularly the periods of technical and economic transformations. And every slowing down of the shifting of economic stratification leads, in due course, to the growth of status structures and makes for the resuscitation of the important role of status honour" [1947(a), p. 193].

Power is exercised in the economy by status groups, although it is formally organised in terms of institutionalised authority and is a social value distributed through the political system; in the case of America and Britain, for instance, through political parties. Such parties may represent interests arising in a class situation or interests that are peculiar to a status group, or both, but as they are social groups themselves to some extent they also represent themselves.

Now the importance of this Weberian analysis is that a system of stratification is seen to depend upon the economic character of society, the way prestige is distributed, and the kind of legal and political institutions it possesses. Here, then, are three criteria, and depending on the kinds of interrelationships between them and their own intrinsic nature, so we may have different stratification systems.

Moreover, Weber's conceptual scheme permits an acknowledgment of the distinction between objective and subjective characteristics. The class situation may be discerned fairly accurately according to objective indices, but the awareness and organisation of strata by members of a society is something quite distinct; differential ranking does not of itself promote what Marx called the "class struggle", for Weber held that although there is subjective consciousness of status it is not necessarily associated with objective indices, and, moreover, it varies among people who share the same class situation. But we may add that this provides no logical reason to claim that because of this fact ranking *cannot* promote the "class struggle", and the fact that status consciousness varies *within* a class does not necessarily mean that this outweighs consciousness of differences *beween* such groups on the part of those within them.

Schumpeter on Class and Family

Different from Weber's and rather more akin to Marx's analysis is that of Schumpeter. This, whilst recognising the distinctions made by Weber between *class* and *status* as useful for analysis, regards them as irrelevant to a less abstract and less analytical approach to the subject (1951). Schumpeter discusses what he maintains is generally recognised as the system of stratification, and so he boldly speaks of *social classes* as groups. He refuses to lay any weight on the similarity of class position of the working man and the professional man, as would a classification in terms of property-holding, for the differences between the two far outweigh the similarities as regards behaviour and outlook.

For Schumpeter classes are aware of their identity, their members behave toward each other in a manner characteristically different from their behaviour toward members of other classes, there is homogeneity in outlook and experience, and the members have similar social interests. Social classes, he argues, are commonly observable phenomena. We might perhaps be inclined to see a similarity between this kind of social class and a status group, for the main feature singled out by Schumpeter is that social classes are endogamous; indeed, it appears that he defines them in terms of this feature.

What interests Schumpeter is social mobility, and it is in examining this that he is led to an understanding of the place of classes in complex society. In the first place, families may rise or fall within a class, and they do so for various reasons. It may be that land that they own appreciates in value over time, a factor underlying the rise, for example, of the Grosvenors, Russells, and Howards in England; or, again, a family which is in a powerful position, both economically and politically, is able to use its favourable position to render it still more favourable, whilst families less fortunately placed are more likely to lose position than gain it within a class; furthermore, families displaying shrewd management and carefully-planned marriage policies advance within their class; or perhaps success and skill in war or favourable opportunities quickly seized provide the reasons for the rise of a family, but by the same token by being unfortunately on the wrong side or by missing the chance may mean a fall instead; and in periods of industrialisation, in particular, the family which saves and invests its savings, whilst living frugally, may so obtain a secure foothold economically that it advances quite rapidly when investment bears fruit.

Now, all these reasons hold when we consider the movement of families over the class barriers, thus providing an explanation for movement between classes, for class barriers are, he says, always surmountable. Schumpeter then continues to comment on the rise of classes in relation to each other. Most obvious as a case in point is the rise of the gentry in the seventeenth and eighteenth centuries, or the middle classes during the industrialisation of England, and particularly that element of them we call the professional class.

Now this examination of social mobility of families and classes enables Schumpeter to offer an explanation of class structure, for he points to personal abilities as the key to upward mobility of families and the function a class performs. Of course, some classes fail to serve their function and are likely to suffer as a result, just as individual families may fail to seize their opportunities, but in so far as they do fulfil their function in the social system and are able to contribute to the maintenance of the system, their position is assured.

Social Functions of Stratification

In the modern urban industrial society, where differentiation is primarily occupational, evaluations to a considerable extent are made of occupational social positions in terms of their function. It is not a perfect evaluation, perhaps, nor is there complete agreement, but the evidence that has accrued shows that there is sufficient agreement by people diversely located to support the view that prestige is distributed according to social worth, or what is thought to be the social worth of occupational positions. Let us look at this more closely.

Firstly, the argument put forward by Davis and Moore (1945) and ably stated and developed by Barber (1957) may be summarised as follows. There are two functions of a system of stratification : one an integrative function, the other adaptive. In so far as there is a differential ranking of social positions, which is an expression of social values, then despite the differences between people that it points to, this ranking in strata serves to help to integrate a society. This is because it enshrines a sense of justice; those who perform the important tasks deserve to be recognised, and prestige is readily accorded them. But also, in order to have accomplished what is necessary, there must be a system of rewards so that social positions are filled and the roles performed adequately. Both material rewards and prestige are accorded differentially so that both integrative and adaptive functions are served. Men value not only the material rewards, but when occupying social positions which are lowly evaluated they nevertheless value them because they serve a social function. This we can see from studies of unemployed men, like those of Bakke (1940) and Morse and Weiss (1955), which show that such men and their families missed not merely the material rewards but the prestige of having a job, prestige which gave them self-respect; for every job has prestige compared with unemployment.

Generally speaking, we may say that the ranking of social positions unequally arises from two sources. Thus Davis argues, on the one hand, there is the necessity to distribute prestige according to the importance to society of a social position, or at least positions of minor importance must not be allowed to compete successfully with ones of major importance, and, on the other hand, that social positions require differential skills, ability, or responsibility from their incumbents (1948). Inherent skills may be scarce and training long and expensive. Thus such social positions requiring preparation must be highly rewarded, and one way of doing so is to evaluate them highly; prestige so accorded stems from a common evaluation (*op. cit.*, Chap. 14).

This argument seeks to explain the universality of ranking. It points to function rather than to cause, for it remains to be shown how differences in systems of stratification occur. To answer this more fully the sociologist has to make a historical study as well, but such historical sociological studies, as MacRae points out in his catholic survey of the literature on the subject, are rare (1953).

The Social Grading of Occupations and Social Classes

Contemporary studies of social stratification focus attention on prestige attached to occupational positions. They combine both an objective and a subjective approach to the subject, asking how far do people perceive occupational positions to be ranked in a hierarchy and to what extent do people, diversely located occupationally, agree in their grading of them. In so far as there is a general agreement it enables sociologists to ask further questions, for example, about voting behaviour in political elections

In England the Department of Sociological and Demographic Research at the London School of Economics has carried out extensive studies in this field. Thus Hall and Jones (1950), as part of these studies of social mobility (Glass, 1954), undertook to discover how occupations were graded. They noticed that various bodies did in fact, for administrative purposes, grade occupations into a few categories. Thus the Registrar-General in 1911 used a fivefold classification: Upper and Middle Class, Intermediate, Skilled Workman, Intermediate, Unskilled Workman. And others, sociologists among them, had similar kinds of classification, as, for instance, that used by the Merseyside Social Survey. Hall and Jones obtained a similar one on their estimate of how social prestige is distributed occupationally. Their "standard classification" was drawn up after examining the degree of training required, the responsibilities and skills involved, and provides for seven classes:

1. Professional and High Administrative.
2. Managerial and Executive.
3. Inspectional, Supervisory, and other Non-Manual, higher grade.
4. Inspectional, Supervisory, and other Non-Manual, lower grade.
5. Skilled Manual and routine grades of Non-Manual.
6. Semi-skilled Manual.
7. Unskilled Manual.

Hall and Jones then selected thirty different occupations, and these were graded by 1,056 people into five classes lettered from A to E. The classes were not defined, except that A was to be regarded as the highest and E the lowest in status. Within each class occupations were to be graded in order also; the tying of occupations judged to be equal was explicitly permitted.

The results showed a remarkable degree of uniformity of judgment, although it must be pointed out that the informants, whilst including men and women of different ages and occupations, were not entirely representative of the occupied population of the country, there being a preponderance of skilled manual and clerical people. Three occupations only appear to have presented a problem. Thus, those of the farmer, coal hewer, and railway porter were placed rather differently in the standard classification as compared with the consensus demonstrated by the empirical findings. Despite this, the agreements between the two were striking. Some occupations were "tied", and it remains to discover precisely what this means, for it may mean that the respondent considered the two tied occupations ranked equally in a prestige hierarchy, but it may mean that he was ignorant of differences between them, or even that the two are incomparable; it is difficult to compare, for instance, a chef with a commercial traveller, or a minister of religion with a works manager, and to tie such occupations may be a way of placing them in a residual category. Social grading of occupations appears to illustrate some homogeneity of opinion about them irrespective of age, sex, or occupation of respondents, although people obviously are better informed about occupations near their own on the scale than those at some considerable remove from theirs.

The next question that the sociologist asks, when occupations have been graded, is how far they are identified with social classes. How are the strata named? How do people identify their own occupation when they use terms like "middle class" or "working class"? Here we are clearly concerned with the subjective aspect of social stratification, and such research as has been carried out in this field does not present us with an unambiguous picture.*

Part of the work carried out by the Department of Sociological and Demographic Research involved a study of Hertford, a small county town, and Greenwich, a metropolitan borough, designed to shed light on political behaviour (Glass, *op. cit.*, Chap. III). Some information was obtained about the subjective aspects of social stratification. It appeared that most people thought in terms of three social classes, which they named "upper", "middle", and "lower" (or "working") class. Some spoke of a "professional class", but identified it with upper middle class. Most people placed themselves either in the middle class or in the working class. However,

---

* Although important investigations into the subjective aspects of social stratification have been carried out in the U.S.A. by W. Lloyd Warner and his colleagues (1942, 1949) it is appropriate here to continue our discussion solely with reference to studies in the U.K.

when occupations were associated with these categories some interesting differences became apparent. Whilst there was unanimity in self-assessment at the extreme ends of the scale of occupations there was a divergence in the middle. The lowest grade of non-manual employees was evenly divided between "working class" and "middle class".

Moreover, there were differences between the two towns. In the county town of Hertford there was a marked propensity for people to cling to middle-class status. Clerks, tradesmen, supervisors, and technicians were, as compared with those in Greenwich, more frequently inclined to think of themselves as middle-class people, and correspondingly less likely to describe themselves as working-class folk. Generally it was found that women were more likely than men to up-grade themselves.

The overall picture showed some marked differences of perspective regarding social placement when people replied to the question: What sort of people belong to the same class as yourself? Those who regarded themselves as middle class were apt to describe the working class as consisting of dustmen, navvies, road-sweepers, and so forth, which are the least esteemed occupations, whilst those whose self-rating was working class hardly ever mentioned these occupations; on the contrary, they tended to mention people whose self-rating frequently was middle class, such as clerks, shop assistants, and so forth. Non-manual workers who rated themselves as working class did, in fact, shift the boundary to include many non-manual workers.

The conclusion is clear. The concept of "middle class" as popularly used is a vague and ill-defined one. Nevertheless, it is obvious that these differences do not denote a lack of class allegiances, for non-manual employees whose subjective status is working class rather than middle class have down-graded other non-manual occupations to their own estimation and set the middle-class boundary at the professional level, just as some manual workers subjectively placing themselves in the middle class include other manual workers also with supervisors and clerks, and regard the professional people as upper class.

This recent research into social stratification in Britain has aimed to discover something about the degree of social mobility present in our society. It has therefore been of particular interest to know what effects changes in the educational system have had upon it. This subject will be treated at some length later, but it is suggested that much of the vagueness about the composition of the middle strata probably stems from the changes that have taken place in recent years as a result of better opportunities for secondary grammar school and higher education, opportunities that bear ultimately on occupational positions. But consideration of social mobility is so dependent on an analysis of the educational system that it is best dealt with separately.

Social Stratification and Political Behaviour

Before bringing this discussion of social stratification to a close it is important to ask to what extent both objective factors like occupation and subjective ideas of status influence the political system and electoral behaviour. This has been the subject of several enquiries, perhaps the most interesting being that of Benney, Gray, and Pear (1956) into the national election of 1950 in Greenwich. These authors, besides using the Hall and Jones scale of occupations, made use of another objective index, namely income; the result was their development of the Social-Economic Status scale, which although primarily taking account of income also includes apparent standard of living and the accent and general bearing of the informant in the assessment of his status.* The way people voted in the election, according to their declaration, was compared with their rating on each of these scales. In both cases the scales showed that the proportion who voted Conservative steadily decreased with each step down the scale whilst the proportion who voted Labour steadily increased. The fourth category on the Hall and Jones scale, namely "Inspectional, Supervisory, and other Non-manual lower grade", were found, however, to vote Conservative even more often than those in the higher prestige grades. The authors hazard an explanation that such people, being on the fringe of the "middle class", feel a need to safeguard their position by a more strict conformity to the norms of that class, and in so doing make up for their financial inability to conform in other ways.

---

* Some disadvantages of using income alone as an index may be seen from the analysis made by Carr-Saunders and D. Caradog Jones (1927) as a result of which these authors misleadingly concluded that classes do not exist.

What does emerge from this study is that one is justified in speaking of two major classes, defined in terms of both income and occupation, for these two objective indices are associated more closely with voting behaviour than are any other variables. Moreover, the authors were able to show that when people assigned themselves to a class, their voting behaviour was closely associated with their subjective class placement. Indeed, there appeared often to be an identification of class with party. It is interesting to note that there was a closer association of subjective placement and party support than the objective indices indicated. And as for the somewhat vaguely defined middle strata they say of these that "subjective views of class position are of most help as predictors of vote in the case of people whose incomes and occupations are on the borderline between middle class and working class" (*op. cit.*, p. 120).

This investigation is interesting for a further reason. It appeared that party supporters, whilst conceding that a particular party served the interests of a particular class, did in a very large number of cases believe that it also served the interests of the other class. There seemed to be a widespread belief in the harmony of interests between classes. Apart from this, however, it must be pointed out that many people on the margin between middle class and working class were not clear about their interests, but these people, we may assume, contain many among them who are socially mobile. An analysis of the political behaviour and ideas of these marginal people is given by Bonham (1954).

Summary and Conclusions

Much more may be said about social stratification, and we shall refer to it again in subsequent chapters. For the present, let us summarise and offer a conclusion. In Britain at least, and there is evidence to show it is broadly true of other complex societies, occupations are ranked and both material rewards and prestige are distributed among them according to their functions for the system and the degree of difficulty in filling occupational positions. There is an awareness of a simple stratified structure and political behaviour broadly corresponds to this class membership. There is mobility between classes, and there is, as we might expect, some ambiguity of belief and behaviour at the margin between middle and working classes. Many people with varying intensity of feeling deplore class differences and egalitarian sentiments are frequently voiced. Despite this, however, there is considerable effort exerted by many people to rise in the social scale. What can we say about this phenomenon?

It may be argued that in the complex society differentiation, particularly in occupational positions, necessarily implies hierarchical ranking. Some positions are functionally more important than others, some are relatively more difficult to fill than others. Both material rewards and prestige are a means for facilitating the process of social life in such a complex society. On the other hand, the stratified system is an open one, and it must be open to permit mobility, so that aptitudes, abilities, and propensities for development may contribute to the maintenance of the social system. Given this kind of social system, economically and internationally competitive, it would seem that there must be stratification.

The kind of system we are considering is one where the structure has to be adaptable to a high degree, as the environment imposes ever fresh demands on it. For the system to persist over time it must be capable of structural change, whilst retaining those features that contribute to its basic stability during each phase of change. As some have put it: the system must be in a state of equilibrium, even if it is a series of moving equilibria. If status is a reward to be won, then class may be regarded as representing interests to be defended. The open class system of this complex society is related to both change and stability. There is a certain interdependence of status and class, for, as we shall see when examining the educational system, class has a bearing on opportunities and education has a bearing on status. And the point of the interdependence lies in the family, which, as Schumpeter rightly pointed out, is the unit of social classes. Given, then, the complex society as we know it, and the family as an important part of the social structure, the system demands that there be stratification not only in terms of occupations but also in terms of families. Occupational status implies social class and social class implies differential political behaviour.

If, as some would have it, egalitarian ideas are to be translated into action, it follows that the social system must be of a radically different type, a type that could dispense with competition both within and without; indeed, it is difficult to see how it could be a social type possessing a complex economy with highly developed administrative structures. But this aspect of the kind of society we have been discussing must now be examined in more detail.

BIBLIOGRAPHY AND FURTHER READING

Bakke, E. W., *Citizens without Work*, 1940 (Yale).
Barber, B., *Social Stratification: A Comparative Analysis of Structure and Process*, 1957 (Harcourt Brace).
Benney, M., Gray, A. P., and Pear, R. H., *How People Vote. A Study of Electoral Behaviour in Greenwich*, 1956 (Routledge and Kegan Paul).
Bonham, J., *The Middle Class Vote*, 1954 (Faber).
Bottomore, T. B., *Classes in Modern Society*, 1965 (Allen and Unwin).
Carr-Saunders, A. M., and Caradog Jones, D., *A Survey of the Social Structure of England and Wales as illustrated by statistics*, 1927 (O.U.P.). Rev. Ed. 1958.
Chapman, D., *The Home and Social Status*, 1955 (Routledge and Kegan Paul).
Davis, K., *Human Society*, 1948 (Macmillan, New York).
Davis, K., and Moore, W. E., "Some Principles of Stratification", *American Sociological Review*, 10, 1945.
Glass, D. V., Ed., *Social Mobility in Britain*, 1954 (Routledge and Kegan Paul).
Hall, J., and Caradog Jones, D., "Social Grading of Occupations", *British Journal of Sociology*, I, 1, 1950.
MacRae, D. G., *Social Stratification: Current Sociology, Vol. II, No. 1*, 1953-4 (U.N.E.S.C.O.).
Marshall, T. H., *Citizenship and Social Class*, 1950 (C.U.P.).
Mitford, N., "The English Aristocracy", *Encounter*, V, 3, Sept. 1955.
Morse, N. C., and Weiss, R. S., "The Function and Meaning of Work and the Job", *American Sociological Review*, 20, 1955.
Pear, T. H., *English Social Differences*, 1955 (Allen and Unwin).
Schumpeter, J., *Imperialism and Social Classes*, 1951 (Blackwell).
Tumin, M. M., *Social Stratification: The forms and functions of inequality*, 1967 (Prentice-Hall).
Veblen, T., *The Theory of the Leisure Class*, 1899, 1949 (Allen and Unwin).

Warner, W. Lloyd, Meeker, M., and Eells, K., *Social Class in America: A Manual for Procedure for the Measurement of Social Status*, 1949 (Chicago).

Warner, W. Lloyd, and Lunt, P. S., *The Status System of a Modern Community*, Yankee City Series, Vol. 2, 1942 (Yale).

Weber, Max, "Class, Status, and Party", *From Max Weber: Essays in Sociology*, Eds. H. Gerth and C. W. Mills, 1947 (*a*) (Routledge and Kegan Paul).

The Theory of Social and Economic Organisation, 1947(*b*) (Wm. Hodge).

CHAPTER VIII

LARGE-SCALE ORGANISATION—SYSTEMS OF SOCIAL STATUS AND COMMUNICATION

If the prestige or social status that a person derives from his occupancy of social positions rests in simple societies upon his place in the kinship system, it rests in complex societies more often upon his place in a working organisation. The most notable feature of complex societies is the large-scale organisation; indeed, the history of complex societies in recent decades has been the progressive and purposive development of social organisations and with them a growth of administrative tasks.

The Structure of Administrative Organisation

Max Weber was one of the earliest sociologists to see the importance of what he called "bureaucracy", and he sought to understand its general characteristics (1947, Chap. VIII). This we referred to in Chapter I, where it was pointed out that Weber discussed both administrative structures and the total socio-economic system of capitalism in terms of ideal types. The new type of administrative structure, or bureaucracy, was, he thought, integral to the development of urban industrial society. This is a generally recognised fact of complex society, irrespective of the politically descriptive title we give to societies; indeed, the terms *capitalist* or *socialist* have become so vague and misleading that they are best dropped; moreover, the phenomena we are concerned with may, in the first instance, be discussed almost without reference to the political arrangements of any one complex society. But whilst attention must naturally be focused on administration, we are also interested in the whole organisational system.

Large-scale organisations with their attendant administrative structures are to-day to be found in the economy, both in its industrial, commercial, and financial manifestations; in government, both central and local; in health and social services; in the educational system at all levels; in professional associations and trade unions; and even in ecclesiastical organisations. Quite obviously, large-scale organisation has developed because it is efficient in achieving the ends purposed, and administrative bureaucracy is so far the best discovered means for maintaining such organisations.

According to Weber, there is in our complex society a rational-legal type of authority where people act according to bodies of purposively defined rules of a general character capable of particular application. These rules define the social positions in corporate groups, their roles and the extent of the authority invested in such positions. In its pure form the bureaucratic administrative staff of an organisation consists of officials who share certain characteristics:

1. They are personally free and subject to authority only with respect to the impersonal obligations of their office.
2. The offices are organised in hierarchical form.
3. Each office has a clearly defined sphere of competence.
4. The office is filled by appointment after selection of the person best fitted for it, and his relationship with the organisation is contractual.
5. Selection is on the basis of technical qualifications.
6. Remuneration is by fixed salary, perhaps with pension rights, but there may be a salary scale.
7. The office is usually the sole occupational position that the incumbent may hold.
8. There is promotion according to seniority and achievement as judged by superiors.
9. The official cannot appropriate his position and does not own the means of administration.
10. The official is subject to discipline and control in the conduct of his office.

The advantages of social positions of this kind are fairly obvious. Continuity of process is ensured as one person succeeds another in office. Specialised tasks may be performed, the general nature and purpose of which are fully understood by those in the organisation. Only those aspects of an individual's life which are relevant to the job are known, or if anything irrelevant is known about an official it is known to be irrelevant. Following from this we may note that administrative processes may take no account of persons, and to

that extent greater calculability may be obtained. Thus, centralised control over a large number of activities and processes may be
achieved. All these things are essential to large-scale organisation.

Formal Organisation

With these introductory remarks let us look at one type of organisation with a view to examining the system of social positions and
at the same time to noting that such a system is also a system of
statuses, *i.e.* a system whereby prestige is distributed in an ordered
form. In any large-scale organisation we shall find what has been

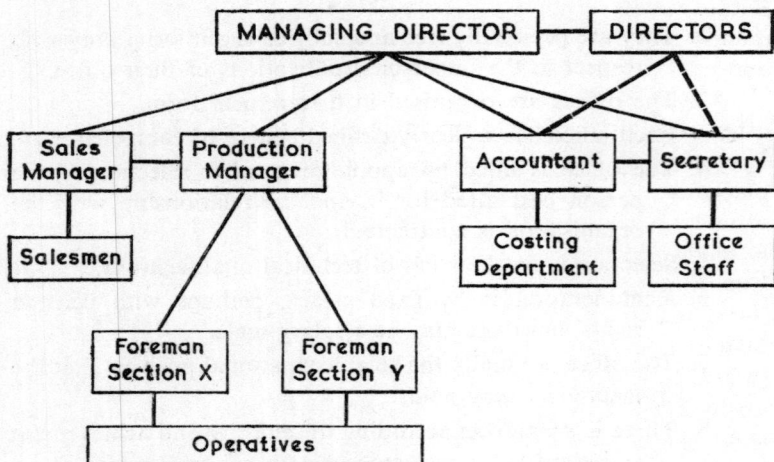

FIG. 7.

called a *formal organisation*, or in other words a structure of social
positions. Business firms are used to using organisational charts to
illustrate the structure; a simple one is set out in Fig. 7.

Such a chart shows various social positions relative to each
other; it shows the chain of command, and thereby it also points
to some extent to the official channels of communication; indeed,
a structure of positions is also largely a structure of communications. Let us first consider the relationships between positions in
such a formally organised structure, examining the implications of
the differential distribution of status, and then proceed to look at
the system of communications.

As C. I. Barnard (1946) has pointed out, nearly all members of organisations are preoccupied with matters of status; people feel it to be important, but we must ask why this is so. To begin with, we can see that the status of a social position is established and maintained by various means, including ceremonies of induction or appointment, insignia, titles, emoluments, and perquisites, and certain kinds of limitations and restrictions regarding both rights and duties. Of course, a man may do a job well or badly, in which case his performance is evaluated in terms of people's understanding of his role. But apart from this the social position itself is evaluated purposively by the people setting up the organisation or those ultimately responsible for its continuance. Status is thus recognised and maintained, and is so partly by the means mentioned above.

All social positions are evaluated, of course, relative to each other. But why is social status imputed to social positions? The answer is somewhat complex. Barnard argues that, in the first place, there is an individual need, particularly if a person has had to make sacrifices and postpone or abandon gratifications in order to qualify for a social position. But, although this is undoubtedly true, we are not here specifically concerned with the psychology of the individual. Secondly, however, he points out that for a command to be obeyed it must come from someone who has authority to give it, and men obey in so far as this authority to command is institutionalised; status higher than that of the recipient of an order is a means of indicating that the person issuing the order does so in terms of the authority vested in him.

It will be appreciated that this term *authority* is somewhat ambiguous, for it may mean that the person giving the order has skills or expertise which give him the authority of superior knowledge, or it may mean that the organisation confers authority on a man, so that he and only he is allowed to give that order. The difference is one distinguished by the terms "functional status" and "scalar status" respectively. Thus we readily accept medical advice from a doctor or nurse, but we would hesitate to do so if it were proffered by an artist or a mechanic, for we recognise the authority of superior knowledge and experience of the doctor in his particular sphere of competence. Technical expertise confers status then, but it is functional status. On the other hand, many commands are usually obeyed only when the person issuing them has that authority

vested in him which we recognise as legitimate. Here status is conferred by a social order based on rules and norms so that he is
recognised as the giver of commands that must be obeyed; this is
scalar status.

The most significant feature of social positions in large-scale
organisations is the frequently impersonal character of communications between their occupants. Status is primarily the status of
office and regulates communication between them. It is not the
practice for communications to be addressed by Mr Smith to Mr
Jones, but rather by the "Manager of Dept. X" to the "Foreman
of Section Y". One obvious advantage of this is that the communication will not follow Mr Jones when he has been removed from
his position as foreman, but will be received by whoever at that
time happens to be the occupant of that position. Of course, very
often there is an identity of functional and scalar status. The
manager may know more than the foreman technically, but then,
not infrequently, he may not. If he is technically inferior we might
ask if his superior status is reasonable, but then we have to remember that he possesses other kinds of knowledge and that this may
be no less technical, for he has a wider grasp of the larger situation
and possesses knowledge about the implications of the work of the
foreman for a larger part of the organisation than the foreman can
comprehend from the limited perspective of the activities of his
section.

It must be pointed out, however, that the functional status of
the foreman as a technical expert will influence the manager less
technically endowed in so far as the foreman sends reports about
the situation in his section; these the manager takes cognisance of,
being aware that the man on the spot is in a better position to know
what is happening than he is. But the manager's actions may still
not be those which his foreman expects, for the manager has wider
interests to serve than those of the section, and the information
passed on to him may well be evaluated differently in the light of
this wider knowledge of the organisation and situations elsewhere
which he must take into account. Nevertheless, it is important to
note that communications proceed both ways, up and down the
hierarchy, down in terms of commands and up in terms of reports
and memoranda.

Scalar status based on differential authority is not a sufficient condition for communications to be maintained. Information of the nature of either command or report must be intelligible. The hierarchy of positions facilitates interpretation of information. Not every person making decisions is *au fait* with all the technical languages used in a large-scale organisation. The research chemist and the accountant may very well not understand the technicalities of each other's work, yet communication must be possible between them. Such communication is mediated. Thus, positions in the organisation are given status in order that information may be communicated in forms that are intelligible and yet in such a manner that authenticity is still maintained. Moreover, status systems are indications for members of an organisation of appropriate language and of interpretive facilities.

To sum up, we can see that status systems in large-scale organisations serve both psychological and sociological functions, that is to say they contribute to the stability and welfare of the individual personality and they serve functions for the organisation of activities and communications. They also have disruptive tendencies and may be dysfunctional, and it is here that we have a sphere where sociology may be applied to practical problems. Barnard's analysis is particularly valuable. He points, in the first place, to psychological problems. Thus social positions are evaluated in terms of their importance, but importance is attributed largely in terms of the scarcity of positions, sometimes irrespective of whether or not they are necessary to the maintenance of the social system. Just as agricultural occupations are highly necessary but possess low status, whilst archaeologists are not essential yet scarce and possess high status, so it may be in an organisation. Social evaluation of what is important, however, is often imputed to the individual as well as to his position, with the result that in some cases it tends to exaggerate the estimate a person has of his worth, either depressing it or enhancing it. In an organisation this means that measures have to be employed to counteract the tendency, restoring morale among some and checking the egoism of others.

What all this means is that modern large-scale organisation has to balance stability and change. It has to foster those processes which give it stability, of which the status system is one, so that local temporary inefficiencies must sometimes be tolerated lest a local efficiency be purchased at too high a price for the organisation as a whole. Thus, to replace one person by another in a social position means loss of some communicability, arising out of the disruption of personal relations well established, until such time as the new occupant has established himself with his colleagues; for impersonality of communications, as we shall see, is not entirely functional. This means restricting mobility which otherwise might serve to enhance efficiency by replacing the less able by the better equipped person. Moreover, the removal of a person from office may be regarded as derogatory to that office, because of the common tendency to identify person and position. Hence the well-known method of promoting to higher status positions those people it is desired to replace by more efficient ones.

Not only is efficiency demanded, but so also is adaptability, for organisations must be capable of altering to meet new needs. Every technological advance means a change in organisation and hence in relationships. Competition, mobility, and careful administrative regulation are all called for to achieve efficiency and adaptability, but the dilemma remains, for if these principles were always carried through the stability of the organisation would be impaired. Status systems are both functional and dysfunctional, but to understand in what respects they are so we have to see them in terms of the parts of the organisation on the one hand, and also of the total social system that the organisation represents on the other hand.

Informal Organisation

So far, in speaking of status systems, we have assumed that social status, as distributed in an organisation, reflects a common evaluation; that what the people responsible for setting up the organisation consider essential in this respect is shared by all those involved. But this is not necessarily the case. Here we must consider informal status in what Barnard calls *informal organisation*, and this must bulk large in a consideration of the functioning of any large-scale organisation (1938).

Following Brown (1954) we may distinguish several different levels at which informal organisation may be found. Firstly, it is pervasive throughout, for, as we have pointed out, there are informal relationships between people formally situated or positioned in the structure which develop naturally and may be encouraged in so far as they facilitate communication. This kind of informal relationship may indeed exist between groups where departmental members meet informally at socials or for work breaks. Secondly, there are large informal groups which may arise as a result of some particular issue in the organisation affecting the welfare or the status of a large number of people; such an informal organisation underlies the formation of a public opinion on a question of some moment. Thirdly, there are the very important *primary groups*, often small and of a face-to-face character, which constitute the actual working groups. There are many of these, and more will be said about them later. Fourthly, there are groups of intimate friends, few in number, perhaps only two or three persons being intimate, feeding together regularly, perhaps sharing common hobbies or leisure-time interests outside the organisation. Lastly, there may be a few isolated individuals who nevertheless from time to time exercise considerable influence on their fellows, perhaps as agitators or critics.

In thus focusing our attention on informal organisation, and in particular on informal social groups, we are able to discern some of the latent functions they serve, for the formal organisation is insufficient as a means to achieving the manifest ends for which it is set up. After all, we know full well that "working to rule" is dysfunctional. There are problems inherent in any organisation which cannot be resolved by the formal organisation by itself without recourse having to be made to other means. The account of aircraft planning during the last war given by Devons, for instance, displays abundant evidence of the importance of informal channels of communication in securing co-ordination between departments and directorates (1950).

The fact that in various groups within an organisation there are differences of status, or unofficial channels of communication, not recognised by the formal organisation, was pointed out by Roethlisberger and Dickson as a result of their studies in the 1930s in the Western Electric Company (1939). These studies, simplified and popularised by Elton Mayo (1949), have shown us that whilst informal groups may sometimes hinder the achievement of the manifest aims of the organisation they are also certainly indispensable for the achievement of them. This is because any working group develops its own norms of behaviour.

Psychologists who undertake studies of small groups, particularly of work groups, do so because they are aware that many individual satisfactions arise from face-to-face interactions, but they also know that the environment of a human group enables the individual to accomplish tasks which by himself he would never complete. Thus Brown emphasises the fact that the primary group is a social instrument conditioning the individual's attitudes, opinions, goals, and ideals. He also points out that it is one of the fundamental sources of discipline and control. One factor to be borne in mind when considering this is that if a group of people derive personal satisfaction through interacting with each other in a group they are likely to enjoy the work they do together and which provides the *raison d'être* for their being members of that group.

Indeed, it seems likely that if large-scale organisations are to persist and achieve their goals efficiently the divorce of working activity and social activity must not be permitted to take place. In a careful assessment of the evidence provided by small group studies Sprott (1958) argues that many people appear to desire closer association in purposive groups in which they would have a sense of significance. But he is also aware that as regards industrial organisation attention to small work groups is not the answer to all industrial problems.

There are often basic divergences of interests underlying labour-management relations, and, of course, the small group may be closely knit in opposition to the aims of the administration. A group of operatives on the same work-bench may develop their individual skills to a point where they satisfy the group norm as to how quickly they work or the amount of their output, and these may be different from those quantities expected by the management, and indeed will frequently be less than those they are capable of. On the other hand, no norm will be reached unless the work group accepts it. Loyalty to the group may mean that output and speed are related to the level of skill of the weaker members of the group rather than the best endowed. Or again, fear of unemployment or a change in the method of production may influence group behaviour. Many incentive schemes have failed to achieve their ends because the goal of high wages ran counter to group norms, as has been variously illustrated by Mayo (*op. cit.*), by Coch and French (1948), and by many other investigators.

In order to avoid the proliferation of examples of studies of the relation of formal and informal organisation we shall give an account of one study, which brings out a number of important points relevant to this general discussion of status and communications. The study we shall refer to was concerned with a method of mining coal in Britain, and draws attention to the relationship of both sociological and psychological factors (Trist and Bamforth, 1951).

Social Organisation in Coal-mining

Among the various methods of securing coal from underground deposits the Longwall method is one which has been tried and on the whole has been found wanting, despite the fact that it involves mechanisation and large-scale operation, features that commend themselves to those interested in increasing production. An examination of the kind of organisation involved is instructive. The method entails a direct advance into the coal on a continuous front; this may mean tackling a coal-face 180-200 yd. wide. The entire process of extracting coal is broken down into a number of operations following each other over three shifts of seven and a half hours each, so that a total cycle of operations is completed every twenty-four hours. In the instance we have taken about forty men are required: on the first shift ten men are engaged on the cutting operation; on the second shift a further ten on the ripping operation; and on the third shift twenty men are engaged on the filling operation.

Let us imagine a coal-face extending ninety yards on either side of a main gate or tunnel to the side gates, respectively "ripped" up to a height of nine and seven feet; the seam of coal may be only three feet thick. Props are placed every three feet to keep up the roof. Where the coal has already been extracted the roof has been allowed to collapse, only the gates being kept open for access to the face and for removal of the coal. On each cycle of operations the coal is hewn out to a depth of six feet, and during each cycle the coal-cutting and removing equipment has to be moved forward. Let us consider the spatial and temporal situation. In the first place a group of men is spread over a distance of 200 yd. in a tunnel two yards wide and one yard high, intersected only by the main and side gates. In the second place the workers are divided by shifts, three in number, succeeding each other within a twenty-four hour period.

The difficulties in communication, both spatially and temporally, are considerable, and as we shall see there are difficulties arising out of the different positions and roles involved and the way social status is distributed. In the Longwall system there are seven main positions: two borers, who bore the holes in which the shot is placed for explosion; two cutters, who use the cutting machine to take out coal at the bottom of the face to a height of six inches along the full extent, one man knocking out props and the other replacing them as the cutter passes along the face and also inserting noggings or blocks to keep up the coal above the under-cut and prevent sagging; four gummers, who clean out the undercut so that when the shot is fired the coal will have space in which to fall and thus break in workable pieces; two belt-breakers, who shift the belt engine up to the face and dismantle the conveyor which is in the old track; two belt-builders, who reassemble the conveyor in its new track; eight rippers, who clear the main and side gates and build up the roof; and twenty fillers, who with hand or air picks each work a part of the face, or stint, clearing the coal, which is then thrown on to the conveyor, and propping the roof as they move forward.

To summarise in terms of the job-processes we may say that there are four stages: preparing the coal-face for firing the shots, shifting the conveyor, work on the main and side gates, and removing the coal. To describe the process in terms of shifts we note that the first shift is concerned with boring the holes, driving the coal-cutter so that it makes an even undercut from the floor, clearing out the "gummings", and belt-breaking. On the second shift the belt-builders reassemble the conveyor, the main and side gates are prepared, and the shot is fired. On the third shift the coal is removed and the roof propped up.

Differences in status between these various workers, as conferred by the formal organisation of the mining industry, are small, and this is reflected in their more or less equal earnings. However, some workers are better than others and some have an easier time than others, particularly fillers, for some fillers may have a stint to work where the coal is more solid than on other stints, and those at the ends by the side gates have an easier time altogether.   But the informal status system sets the gummers lower than others in status, and indeed they are often the objects of criticism for many faults.   The front man on the cutter and the main ripper have a higher status than others of their kind.   The one man who has some responsibility for the cycle as a whole is the deputy, but his status, it appears, is often incommensurate with his responsibilities.   Thus we may point to the difficulties of communication between management and men which are mediated by the deputy.

Moreover, the three shifts are separate but dependent on each other for their success.   Indeed, the shifts may never meet, for the system is such that when two shifts are off duty one shift is probably asleep.

Again, when we consider the natural difficulties in coal-mining, the damp, heat, dust, and physical disabilities like fatigue and age, and the unexpected hindrances to smooth working as when faults occur in the coal-face or the occurrence of patches of coal which are hard to work, it is not surprising that poor communications aggravate the social and physical problems that are bound to arise. Thus, if the cutters fail to make an even cut, or the gummers fail to clear out the undercut adequately, or the borers fail to ensure that the shot breaks up the coal cleanly, the succeeding stages of the process are adversely affected.   The success of one shift depends on the success of the preceding one, and in turn influences the success of the next.   Even on the third shift, where the fillers, each with his official stint, may be differentially favoured by the conditions they face, it is difficult to secure stability for informal social groups whereby mutual assistance is given—the more fortunately placed helping the less well placed.   Sometimes a cutter or a gummer may be bribed by a filler, with a drink on a Sunday, to ensure a good deal of his own length on his own shift.   But apart from such dubious practices the insecurity of informal organisation means that at many points the system is inadequate.   Intrigue, especially with deputies, and criticism of other shifts is common. When the situation becomes unbearable absenteeism is found to be a way out.   But all these ways of coping with the difficulties merely exacerbate them.

In discussing the problems involved in this method of coal-mining, Trist and Bamforth argue the case for the development of formal small-group organisation, particularly on the filling shift. They also suggest that multiple role playing be encouraged, so that a man is trained and enabled to do more than one task, thus cutting down the time wasted on bottlenecks, but also providing for understanding and personal knowledge of the difficulties faced by people playing different roles. It must not be supposed that in the British mining industry these problems are unknown or that no experiments are being made or different methods employed, but there are besides the technical problems those arising out of the social organisation of the work, and the above illustration is some indication of their importance.

The Relationship of Formal to Informal Status

In examining large-scale organisation we may focus our atten-tion on the formal organisation of social positions, noting the way in which social status is distributed; the system of communica-tions, bearing in mind that decision-making depends for its success on adequate information being available; and the informal organi-sation, both as regards the formation of groups and the overlay of social distinctions and evaluations which follows from the distribu-tion of informal status. Here, then, are some guiding ideas for the understanding of the social processes that occupy a large part of modern industrial social life.

If we were to indicate one of the most important and yet one of the most difficult aspects of social organisation in our society, it would be the relation between informal and formal social status within the organisation and the relationship between these two and the general stratified system of the whole society. The fact is that here is a field, of the nature of which we are largely in ignorance at present. But it is becoming clearer that many of the practical problems of modern society stem from actions which infringe the sense of what people consider to be their due.

Indeed, in so far as prestige or social status is a primary factor in contributing to the satisfaction of both individuals and groups, we may point to the necessity of so arranging matters that people do not have their self-esteem injured by actions which tend to lower the estimation others have of them, and this may occur whenever social positions are differentially treated either by directly altering a social position or altering others in relation to it. In so far as income, which is a reward for work, is affected, not only gross income received but differentials between incomes received have a bearing on such satisfactions.

Moreover, a social system which fails to permit information, both about how people perceive these things and what symbols of informal status exist, from reaching those responsible for it is under severe disadvantages. In other words one task of a sociologist is to be able to understand what kinds of status systems and systems of communication are in fact functional for social organisations, and what kinds may be dysfunctional for them.

BIBLIOGRAPHY AND FURTHER READING

Barnard, C. I., *The Function of the Executive*, 1938 (Harvard).
    "Functions and Pathology of Status Systems in Formal Organisations", *Industry and Society*, 1946, Ed. W. F. Whyte (McGraw Hill).

Blau, P. M., and Scott, W. R., *Formal Organizations*, 1963 (Routledge and Kegan Paul).

Brown, J. A. C., *The Social Psychology of Industry*, 1954 (Pelican).

Coch, L., and French, J. R. P., "Overcoming Resistance to Change", *Human Relations*, I, 1948.

Devons, E., *Planning in Practice: Essays in Aircraft Planning in War-time*, 1950 (C.U.P.).

Mayo, E., *The Social Problems of an Industrial Civilization*, 1949 (Routledge and Kegan Paul).

Roethlisberger, F. J., and Dickson, W. J., *Management and the Worker*, 1939 (Harvard).

Sprott, W. J. H., *Human Groups*, 1958 (Pelican).

Trist, E. L., and Bamforth, K. W., "Some Social and Psychological Consequences of the Longwall Method of Coal-Getting", *Human Relations*, IV, 1, 1951.

Weber, M., *From Max Weber: Essays in Sociology*, 1947, Eds. H. Gerth and C. W. Mills, Chap. VIII (Routledge and Kegan Paul).

CHAPTER IX

SOCIAL ORGANISATION: SYSTEMS OF INTERACTION

In the last chapter we described some of the features of large-scale social organisations, but we also found it necessary to refer to the informally organised relationships between people, especially in work groups. In this chapter we shall continue to examine the nature of social organisation, but from a rather different angle. Whilst we shall be considering the factors of social status and communication we shall also focus attention rather more on the way in which the structure of an organisation affects the behaviour and attitudes of its members. Moreover, we shall be considering different kinds of social organisations. Some of them will be quite small in size; indeed, we might well call them social groups. Thus we shall make some observations about the family and about committees; it will be seen that these are not the same kind of organisations as, say, the business firm or a government department, although they do have some resemblance to the kinds of relationships which we discussed in our last example, a work group. But before saying something about social groups let us consider a type of social organisation which has been described by Erving Goffman (1961) as a *total institution*.

Total Institutions

There are five varieties of this type of organisation which we may list as follows:

1. Those that care for persons who are considered incapable but harmless, such as Orphanages and Old People's Homes.

2. Those which care for incapable persons who constitute a threat to society such as Tuberculosis Sanatoria, Mental Hospitals, and Leprosoria.

3. Those which protect society from persons who are considered to be intentional dangers to that society like Prisons and Borstals.

4. Those which are designed to perform technical tasks such as Army Barracks and Ships; and we may include Boarding Schools.

5. Those which are established to achieve religious ends such as Monasteries and Convents.

What these organisations have in common is a tendency to embrace all aspects of the lives of those members which we describe as the inmates. This can be seen in the difficulties of communication between those people inside and those outside, for there may be guards, locked doors, or walls which intentionally prevent social intercourse with the outside. There may be the barrier of the sea or physical isolation on land which naturally prevents easy communication. Now such social organisations are numerous, as well as varied; they constitute a significant feature of our society; they may be regarded as social systems.

Goffman's main interest was in mental institutions but he is well aware that the typical features of mental institutions are often found in other types of social organisations. Other writers have written about social organisation in ships, in boarding schools, and in prisons; all these studies have contributed to our sociological understanding of human society. Let us try to discern the general features of such total institutions. Firstly, in this kind of social organisation the various activities and aspects of a person's life are concentrated under one authority; a person does not live in one place, work in another, and take his recreation in a third place as most of us do. Secondly, his activities are shared with a group of others, which is always the same group, and all the time; what is more all are treated in the same fashion. Thirdly, all the activities follow a tight and regular schedule and, furthermore, these activities tend to be brought under a single rational plan designed to fulfil the official ends of the organisation. It follows there is little room if any for individuality and, indeed, there is a staff whose duty it is to maintain control by watching for and correcting any deviation from the required norms of behaviour.

This last point brings into relief the main feature of such organisations, namely that there is a staff who manage and a body of inmates in whose custody they are; the former group is relatively small, operates on a shift system, and is integrated with the outside world, the latter is cut off and lives wholly within the organisation, except for very restricted and controlled relationships with the outside, slender in content and infrequent in occurrence. The result of these conditions is that staff and inmates tend to perceive each other in hostile terms, the staff are perceived to be high-handed and mean, the inmates are perceived to be unreliable and secretive; staff see themselves as superior, inmates see themselves as weak and often as blameworthy or even guilty, certainly as inferior.

In his description of the behaviour of these two groups Goffman, in general terms, points to the lack of social mobility between them, the maintenance of formally instituted social distance, the control and restriction of communication and especially the tendency to prevent communication between those high in the staff hierarchy and the inmates. The result is the creation of two worlds, in fact two cultures. The total institution is organised in such a manner that it is incompatible with significant features of the external world. Thus, for example, it is not possible, without gross distortions, to introduce the work-payment structure of the wider society, for labour is either punitive or therapeutic, or else it is merely an escape from boredom; moreover, there is a lack of that essential element of contract which is found in normal working conditions.

The kind of analysis underlying the above general description is based on reports and researches, and on autobiographies such as that of T. E. Lawrence,* or former Prisoners of War, or ex-convicts. Goffman has shown it is possible to go on to describe in general terms both the inmate world and the staff world, and the nature of the contacts between the two. It is an analysis of a structure of social relationships, of beliefs and attitudes, of values and of interaction. Such an analysis will help us to understand better the processes of social life. One of the chief features of the interaction of people in a total institution is the process whereby an inmate is systematically stripped of his or her external roles, roles which served to maintain an integrity of the self. On admission, deliberately or otherwise, the inmate is subjected to a series of humiliations and degradations. The process may begin with a medical examination, continue with a replacement of clothes by a uniform, induction into standardised role behaviour patterns in conformity with rules, and these frequently include acquiring a deferential attitude towards

* *The Mint*, 1955.

staff members, personal possessions are replaced by a few standardised institutional ones, and so on and so forth.   Of course the nature and severity of these deprivations varies from one kind of institution to another, but the ingredients are usually all present, whatever the mix.   In some such total institutions there may be considerable brutality of treatment to secure submission, in others there is a more subtle process of subjugating the inmate, often for his own good, to the régime;   many have to suffer in order to receive beneficial treatment.   To pursue this subject further we could examine in more detail a particular total institution.   However, instead of taking in turn a mental hospital, a prison, and so forth, let us consider one which stands a little on the periphery, the life of a ship's company.

The Social Structure of a Ship

Two sociologists, Aubert and Arner (1959), on the basis of statistics, laws, documents, and informants' statements made an analysis of the social structure of ships sailing under the Norwegian flag.   As in other total institutions seamen live and work in the same place, their social intercourse is limited to those on the ship for they are separated from their families and friends ashore.   But there is one interesting fact about a ship's crew: the turnover is much larger than it is in most industrial concerns, so that for any one person a berth is relatively temporary.   Social positions on board are specialised, and few are in a similar position to others. Moreover, the method of payment and the lines of job demarcation are such as to reinforce this particularity.   A seaman's social environment consists of other seamen with whom he is in a formal working relationship and so there is a practice whereby they address one another by the terms describing their position: "Bosun", "the Third", "the Cook", etc.   The high turnover makes it advantageous to stick to titles in addressing shipmates, and as they are fairly specific and there are few with the same job description, this practice is easily maintained.   In the large tankers especially there are separate messing arrangements for the captain, the officers, the petty officers, the crew, and even sometimes for the galley hands; thus a rigid social segregation is maintained.

Friendships are not easily formed, close ones are discouraged, but instead a general comradely behaviour is held to be desirable.

One reason for the lack of close friendships is the rapid turnover, but another stems from the closeness of contact and the importance of getting on with all one's fellows rather than risking the ups and downs of a close friendship where too many confidences may be offered and received and perhaps regretted. A seaman can leave his ship when in port, but he is likely to be there for only a short time. His life centres on the ship where he is in a dependent relationship with his seniors, and yet despite this dependence he is expected to act maturely and in a responsible manner. Aubert and Arner argue that it is in this rather ambivalent attitude to responsibility that we may discern the reason why so many dissatisfied seamen nevertheless remain at sea instead of trying to settle ashore. But we may also note certain stabilities arising out of early upbringing and environment. Thus men from the Shetland Isles and other isolated places tend to become seamen in British ships, and it may well be the case with many Norwegian seamen. Space does not permit a more extensive analysis, but some idea of the way in which a sociologist may analyse an occupation set within a certain kind of social organisation has been given. Suffice it to say that Aubert and Arner go on to discuss the nature of the instabilities of the social group on board ship, the high degree of turnover, the nature of role differentiation, and the way barriers are formed to restrict interaction on board. But let us now leave this particular type of social organisation in order to look at another and contrasting one.

The School Class

Although in the next chapter we shall examine the educational system it is convenient to include in this one a discussion of the social organisation of the school, and especially the school class. Our purpose in this short section is to concentrate on the school in order to show how it may be described as a system of positions and roles. However, we must note at the outset that the school is part of a wider organisation. Thus the state school is connected both to the education office of the local authority, which supervises its activities, and to the Department of Education and Science which periodically inspects it and which regulates through Institutes of Education the training of teachers. Indeed, it has been argued that these connections are such that the role of the school teacher in the school is severely restricted, that he cannot teach precisely what he would like to teach or in quite the way he would wish to teach, with the consequence that he is less free as a professional person than members of other professions. Moreover, as we mentioned in Chapter II when discussing *role-set* a teacher has parents as well as children to consider, members of the local community as well as his headmaster; all of whom attempt to influence him to do what they wish. The school is clearly an organisation which has many relationships with persons and organisations in the wider society and the school teacher also has to try to reconcile influences bearing upon him from inside and outside the walls of the school buildings. Here lie some of the problems that interest the sociologist of education.

Is the school a total institution? Clearly the day school is not, although if it is a boarding school we might consider it to be one. Yet since even a day school has custodial functions, to this extent it has a partial resemblance to a total institution. On the whole, however, we would be inclined to say it is community-orientated, for both children and teachers live in the same community, they usually only meet during school hours, which are working hours, and there are vacations of some length when the school is dispersed. Let us observe also that in the school and within the classroom this wider society is represented and indeed in the classroom the models of roles played outside in the wider community are held up before the children. Some of these models are occupational roles such as scientist, clerk, bus driver, engineer, and so forth. Other models refer to familial roles, neighbourhood roles, citizenship, and so forth. This is a function that all schools perform although of course the actual content will vary from one country to another, and from one culture to another. Moreover, the school classroom is where a child not only learns about adult roles but learns also how to perform them. The ingredients of education, literacy, and numeracy, are imparted in the child as are also minor manual skills like drawing, making things in wood or metal, cloth or wool.

One significant feature of the role structures of the school child lies in his relationships with the school staff. When he is an infant in primary school he will probably have only one teacher, who will teach him everything he has to learn at that age; but in a junior school he will move from one classroom to another, although he may have one which is his base, the form-room. This moving from one classroom to another, as he changes from one subject to another, means a change of teacher, for at this stage in his school career his teachers specialise in particular subjects or groups of subjects, and this of course continues and becomes even more marked as the child proceeds up the educational ladder.

The manner adopted by a teacher, his or her style and method, may vary from one person to another. Some teachers are popular, some less so. The variation in style and method is considerable; this represents variations in role-playing. Such evidence as exists does not make it clear which kind of manner on the part of the teacher is most successful. Some popular teachers, it would appear, are less effective than some unpopular ones. The processes of interaction between teacher and pupil are very complex. Thus Davidson and Lang (1960) discovered that children in primary school who were aware of their teacher's feelings had a higher estimate of themselves, a better school achievement and, according to the teacher, were better behaved in class. Usually, the teacher who wins the confidence and admiration of the class is most success-ful, but we cannot generalise with confidence on this topic. Lippitt's famous studies of authoritarian and democratic leadership in youth club groups carried out in the U.S.A. over thirty years ago suggests that extremes of either kind may be successful in terms of output, although the nature of the relationship varied. Thus matched groups of boys making masks were supervised, one by an adult leader who adopted *laissez-faire* methods and the other by one who used authoritarian methods, directing by telling the boys what to do rather than soliciting their ideas. Indeed, as long as the authori-tarian leader remained in the room the group of boys under this kind of supervision displayed greater productivity than other groups with different leadership styles. (See Lewin, Lippitt, and White, 1939.) Although the present state of research into this question leaves much to be desired it is quite clear that it is in the interaction between teacher and pupil that the answer lies as to how learning may be communicated and enquiry stimulated. But it has to be remembered that communication and stimulation in the classroom depend mostly on language and the kind of studies carried out by Bernstein (Halsey *et al. op. cit.*) into the relationship of social class and linguistic development is highly germane to this topic. There are, in short, certain formal relationships defined by norms relating to the interaction of pupils and teachers, within the structure of the school class and the school itself, and also the community which is the school's environment, but there are also informal relationships, of the kind we discussed in the last chapter, and these are no less important; they stem from the personality and methods of the teacher; and the social background and character of the children and the kind of linguistic expression they are used to.   This brings us to a consideration of the family, which is the prime agency for bringing up the child, itself a social system of great importance.

The Family

Yet is the family of such great importance?   Is it not the case that it has been declining in significance since it has become smaller in size?   And have not schools taken over many familial functions, so that it is now reduced to a small group of parents and children who often have little to do with each other after infancy?

What are the functions of the family as an organisation or social group?   Parsons argues that it has two main functions: firstly, it is a means whereby individuals develop their personalities —a psychological function; secondly, it provides a means for socialising children.   Now when we compare the family to-day with the family of the Victorian era or earlier, we could say that it has lost many of its functions.   To some extent this may be true, although unfortunately and unnecessarily it has led some sociologists to take a very pessimistic view of the family and its place in modern society.   Yet Parsons and Bales argue that those functions which have been retained have become more important than ever before (1955).

The fact that the middle-class family is independent largely of kinsfolk, although economically dependent on the earnings of the head of the household, lends weight to the view that it is more compact, and whilst smaller is also a more cohesive unit.   We might point to the growing practice both in Britain and America of house purchase as supporting evidence for this contention.

Personalities are not born, they are "made" and developed in the socialising process, through the child's interaction with parents, of the same and opposite sex, and with siblings.   This process does not suddenly cease, never to continue, just because a child becomes an adult.   For the individual personality to become mature there must continue to be social interaction with others, and it may be claimed that the best opportunities are offered for this development if the interaction is within the family group, *i.e.* within the social and sexual relationship of marriage.   Given, also, separate occupational roles, highly specialised, requiring for their performance a disciplined training and demanding from the individual considerable sense of responsibility, we may see the family as serving the function of maintaining the stability of the personality.   It seems reasonable to suppose that some sphere, sharply demarcated from the occupational sphere, should be available within which the individual may retire to relax and recreate his energies.   The family with its diffuse and informal relationships permits this to a high degree.   Parsons also suggests that it is necessary for people to have an opportunity to act out their less mature and infantile impulses, impulses which are a part of everyone's make-up.   He goes on to say that children are important to a married couple precisely because they enable them to express the childish elements in their own personalities by interacting with the children on their own, naturally, childish level.

The subtle nature of the relationships between adult men and women in their families, both between themselves and with their children, would appear to provide both stabilisation of adult personalities on the one hand, and to be conducive, on the other hand, to the rearing of children, educating them in a knowledge of the roles appropriate to their sex, and introducing them to the roles played in the wider society outside the family.

The complex society of to-day places a heavy burden on the family.   The very complexity of the social structure implies that the socialisation process must be both long and successful.   It is not insignificant, as Titmuss (1953) has pointed out, that to-day parents are told by teachers, doctors, health visitors, social workers, parentcraft experts, and a host of other people that they owe everything to their children.   Parenthood is rapidly becoming a highly self-conscious vocation, and seen to be a heavy responsibility.   Clearly, the middle-class family will, to meet the demands of this situation, firstly enclose itself within its own household and restrict contacts with the outside world, and secondly will deliberately restrict the number of its children to a figure below what it might have and did have in the past.

We might with some confidence assert that, far from disintegrating, the family has become more important by virtue of the functions it does serve.   Thus, although some people are inclined to see in the higher divorce rates in Britain and America signs of the breakdown of the family, these figures, if they show anything at all, may be indications of the greater demands made on marriage as an institution and the family as a social group, as Mead has argued for America (1950); at least we may discount the view that these higher rates reflect an increase in "broken homes" (McGregor, 1957).

Now it may be argued that this reliance on the family is not limited to middle-class people.   In fact, the development of both statutory and voluntary social services, the ubiquitous influence of the radio, television, the Press, and particularly women's magazines, has led to powerful pressures being put on families of all classes to conform to certain norms.   The fields of education and health, especially, have been productive of new ideas and practices, subsidisation in a variety of forms has had its effects, and in Britain a sharp improvement in the standards of child care has been very noticeable.   What we have said of middle-class families is by no means limited to these, but extends to a broad section of working-class families.   But having said this we must also point to some cultural differences separating some working-class families from others and from middle-class families.   The evidence produced by British sociologists in the 1950s of family structure in Coventry (Kuper, 1953), Oxford (Mogey, 1956), Bethnal Green (Young and Willmott, 1957) and other places is highly instructive.   Townsend (1957), for instance, usefully distinguishes the "immediate family" from the "extended family".   The former represents the small conjugal family of parents and children, the latter term denotes "a group of relatives, comprising more than the immediate family, who live in one, two or more households, usually in a single locality, *and who see each other every day, or nearly every day*" (*op. cit.*, p. 108).   Such an extended family consists of three generations usually, *i.e.* grandparents, their married children, and their grandchildren; less usually, if the grandparents are dead, it may consist of two or more immediate families, particularly two married sisters and their families.

This extended family is a fairly common phenomenon among working-class people, and especially where there is little geographical mobility. Townsend found it to be common in East London for in his investigation into the social life of old people he says of those he interviewed that they had "an average of thirteen relatives within a mile and they saw three-quarters of all their children, both married and unmarried, once a week, as many as a third of them every day" (*ibid.*, p. 205). In Bethnal Green he found that of his sample of old people 58 per cent. belonged to a three-generation extended family. Mogey, writing about the residential district of St. Ebbe's in Oxford, says that there was a set of blood relatives on hand for about half the population (*op. cit.*). Kerr found in Liverpool not only many extended families, but also a large number of married daughters, together with their families, who were living with their mothers. Indeed, matrilocality was, she claims, a significant feature of the area she studied (*op. cit.*). On a temporary new housing estate on the outskirts of Liverpool, erected during the war, the writer himself discovered many grandparents living near their married children, although the method of allocating houses was supposed to favour young married couples, and this was in addition to numerous cases where grandparents lived with their children in a three-generation household (Mitchell and Lupton, 1954).

Although our knowledge of middle-class families is slight, or at least is poorly documented, it seems reasonable to suppose that this extended type of family is not so common. Certainly there does not appear to be the same degree of emphasis in middle-class families on mother-daughter relationships, as Kerr points to in the working-class area in Liverpool, and Young and Willmott indicate with regard to East London. The married daughter, we are told by these writers, receives from her mother not only advice and support in the large personal crises of life, but also much help in the innumerable small domestic affairs of every day. The working-class mother and daughter have much to share, they are both involved in the child-rearing function, the grandmother extending, rather than transferring, her maternal interest from her daughter to her grandchild. Doubtless, this happens occasionally in middle-class families, but it is by no means common; the traditional norm is one of non-interference.

Traditionally, the working-class man tried to avoid being caught up in the close relationship between his wife and her mother. He spent most of his free time with his friends or at the pub. To-day there appears to be a tendency toward more involvement in the family. Yet Young and Willmott point out that a husband is drawn into contacts more with his wife's mother than with his own (*op. cit.,* p. 49 ff.). Moreover, whilst there is contact between siblings, it is not so frequent as the contact a man has with his wife's parents. There is thus some evidence that the working-class family has a tendency to being matriarchially orientated. By contrast, the middle-class family would appear usually to be an "immediate family", as Townsend puts it: more mobile and with fewer and less intense relationships with grandparents and husband's or wife's siblings. And this would seem to be the case, according to Parsons (1955), among the middle-class population in America, but again, by contrast he points to the evidence of a mother-centred type of family structure among lower-class white and negro people.

These remarks about the family as an organisation or group focus our attention on its environment, for the family is part of a neighbourhood, which may be defined as a number of persons including family groups living in physical proximity and who interact with one another. Let us turn, now, to this subject and in particular refer to that large two-volume work by J. Klein (1965) which tried to bring together within a single conceptual framework a number of studies carried out in Britain on the subject of family and neighbourhood.

Neighbourhood Groups

Even in a relatively small country like England there are many local differences, differences in ways of life, customs, attitudes, and outlook. They are perpetuated in the group through the agency of the family, the primary socialising agency, but families are embedded in a social environment. Klein refers mainly to three English community studies: an area in Paddington, another neighbourhood in Liverpool, and a small mining town in Yorkshire, but she also makes reference to other studies carried out since World War II. The three main studies are all odd, in the sense that they are of social situations which lie out of the main stream of English national life. They are compared and contrasted with other studies which describe how the majority of people live, and in this respect most of her book is about the differences between a working-class culture and a middle-class culture, with a description of how working-class life

changes from its traditional pattern in some respects, especially with
the rehousing of populations since World War II and the necessity
for massive post-war housing development.   It is not possible to do
more than pick up a point here and there in this very extensive
analysis, but for the purposes of this chapter it is useful to focus
attention on changes in interaction in neighbourhood groups and
in families.   Young and Willmott had noticed difficulties experienced by Bethnal Green people on being rehoused in a new council
estate (1957) as also did Mitchell and Lupton, where people in
Liverpool had moved to the outskirts (*op. cit.*).   What these
observers, and others too, note is that there is a division in the
working-class community between those who hold the traditional
values, or who are in Mogey's terms "status-assenting", that is they
accept their lot and like the close neighbourly relationships such as
are found among the Bethnal Green inhabitants and who live in
down-town traditional working-class districts, and those who occupy
houses on the post-war housing estates, who have aspirations for
themselves, or at least for their children, and are "status-dissenting".
What is true for working-class people is true also for middle-class
people.   We may distinguish in both categories a traditional section and a mobile section, and their habits and attitudes tend to
differ.   This has a direct bearing upon relationships in a neighbourhood, where patterns of interaction may vary greatly.

One study which sheds some light on this subject is that of
Elizabeth Bott (1957); it is a small scale but intensive study of
the kinds of relationships married couples have with each other
and the kinds of relationships they have in the community.   She
makes use of role analysis in examining the patterns of interaction.
Thus she introduces the terms "conjugal roles" and "social networks".   In regard to the former she examines the nature of the
domestic roles of husbands and wives.   She distinguishes cases
where there are clearly defined, separate, and yet *complementary*,
familial activities;   those where the activities of the spouses are
different and are carried out *independently* without reference one
to the other;   and those where the spouses do things together, have
no clear role-differentiation, and generally act *jointly*;   these are
analytical types of family organisation.   Obviously, all types may
be found in any one family, but in concrete instances she found
the relative emphasis to vary greatly.   In some families the comple-

mentary and independent types were found to predominate, and here she speaks of *segregated conjugal role-relationships.* In such families the husband and wife each have their own domestic and occupational tasks, they expect to have their own recreational pursuits and to have their own friends. Other families display a predominantly joint organisation and may be described as having *joint conjugal role-relationships.* Here the spouses carry out many activities in common, plan things together, and share tasks without clearly differentiating roles according to sex.

Now most families live in a residential environment. Spouses each have relationships outside the family with friends, relatives, neighbours, clubs, community centres, shops, clinics, places of work, pubs, and so forth. These relationships constitute a network. Such networks may themselves be connected to varying extents, *i.e.* the people known by a husband or wife may themselves, and independently of the spouses, be connected with each other. In this connection Bott speaks of "close-knit" and "loose-knit" networks. Her principal hypothesis is that the degree of segregation in the role-relationship of husband and wife varies directly with the connectedness of the family's social network. She argues that the more connected the network the greater the degree of segregation of roles and vice versa. Her empirical work supports this contention.

But how do we explain this? The answer seems to lie in the way in which a social group, whose members interact frequently, develops norms exercising close control over the members' behaviour; a generalisation dealt with at length by Homans (1951) and Klein (1956). If spouses come to marriage with closely-knit networks, providing the physical conditions of the environment permit it, they will continue to be drawn into the activities of these networks, and they will continue to derive certain emotional satisfactions from them—satisfactions which need not then be provided so much within the family itself. Conversely, if they come to marriage with loose-knit networks, there will be less social control from outside and more will be demanded by them from their marriage; in which case joint organisation of the family is likely to predominate. The former type case is not uncommon. It describes the family whose members have grown up in the place surrounded by kinsfolk and friends, where there has been little or no mobility, either of a geographical or a social kind, and where marriage is merely imposed on an existing set of social relationships.

Networks become loose-knit when people move from one place of residence to another some considerable distance away. Much, of course, depends on whether the spouses each moved prior to marriage or whether they moved after. If before, they will have already brought loose-knit networks with them, they will perhaps be stabilised in them, and thus such networks may persist. But in any case they will set high standards of conjugal compatibility, they will stress shared interests, there will be joint organisation and a sense of equality. And all this will obtain because they are not so bound by norms of groups outside the family and because they are necessarily thrown on to their own resources.

It is clear that in moving from one type of social situation to another (and this may well occur on the occasion of marriage itself) there is a difficult process of adjustment. It is perhaps scarcely surprising, therefore, that on new housing estates, very often the only places where newly-married couples can set up a home, privacy assumes the importance that it does, and that the advent of children should emphasise rather than diminish its importance. Moreover, much depends on the quality of social organisation in neighbouring families, for incompatibilities obviously aggravate the difficulties of adjustment, no less so for the help that neighbours can and do give to each other and, furthermore, that they may want to give to each other.

The quality of family life, seen in terms of conjugal roles and the connectedness of networks, is influenced by an overlay of other factors. These have been discussed by the authors we have cited. There are, of course, the personalities of people to be considered, but there are a number of sociological factors, too. Briefly, we may indicate the economic and occupational circumstances of the family, the ecology of the residential setting, the character of social organisations in the neighbourhood and the extent of social provision, and the social class composition of the population.

Social organisation when applied to the neighbourhood and the residential community becomes a very broad category. On the one hand it may be restricted to the pattern of interaction between a few people or a few families. Leon Festinger and his associates found this in their study of a housing estate established by the Massachusetts Institute of Technology to house veterans turned students after World War II (Festinger, Schachter, and Back, 1950). Here the authors focus attention on friendship groupings and the way the layout of the estate affected the interaction of people and furthermore they point to their effect in influencing attitudes. On the other hand social organisation is a term which can be applied to a much larger collection of families, inhabiting a greater area than a housing estate: the study of a Canadian suburb called Crestwood Heights by Seeley, Sim, and Loosley (1956) shows this. Such a study is less concerned with the grouping of people in neighbourhoods than in the way they interact in a community of some size and complexity, the manner in which their lives follow a pattern, in conformity with certain values, aspirations, and compulsions. It becomes a critique of modern urban and suburban culture. In this chapter, however, we have restricted the meaning of the term to interaction in a social group—a ship, a family, a neighbourhood group. It is clear, however, that it may be applied to other forms of human interaction, such as a committee, which is a social group having considerable formality of structure, occupying less of a person's life-space, and whilst often regular probably less permanent than many social organisations. Before we leave the subject of social organisation, let us briefly examine some of the aspects of a committee.

The Committee—a small group organisation

To begin with a committee is a task-oriented organisation of people. It is also formally structured, although the extent to which it is so may vary considerably. However, it is usual for a committee to have a chairman and also a secretary or rapporteur who will make a written record of the principal items of discussion or at least of the decisions arrived at. All this is well known, but it is rather less well known that the behaviour of the members is likely to follow certain well established lines, despite the age of the members, their sex, the nature of their task, and their own individual interests. Thus observations of groups shows that certain functions are performed, the distribution of these functions being informal and automatic largely according to personality. Much of our information about committees is derived from studies of experimental groups, and investigators tell us that certain roles are necessary for the efficient functioning of a social group like a committee engaged in attaining a goal or accomplishing a task; roles like that of innovator, critic, expert, diplomat, elucidator, morale builder, and so forth.

There are various ways of looking at a small group such as a committee, one of which is to see it as a number of persons communicating with each other, exchanging information and assembling it until the solution to a problem is found. In such a process some members make suggestions, some ask for information, some draw conclusions, some encourage, others criticise. It is well known that some people are better committee men than others, and what this means is that some people are more interested in helping the group to achieve its ends than they are to satisfy their own personal inclinations. Thus in every group there may be said to be *task-oriented behaviour*, where people make suggestions, or offer relevant information or help toward the task, and *expressive behaviour*, where people express pleasure or hostility, make pleasing remarks or destructive ones. Such expressive behaviour may satisfy something in the individual or it may be of help to the group, or both. Of course expressive behaviour which is not helpful is likely to affect morale adversely; on the other hand a cohesive group will be able to control the behaviour of its members. R. F. Bales (1950) has devised a schedule to assist observation of group behaviour. Thus examination of the behaviour of any given group attempting to solve a task may be analysed and the part played by the various members may be assessed. These categories are such that each item of behaviour can be classified in such categories as, for example, *shows solidarity, shows tension-release, gives opinion, gives orientation, asks for suggestions, disagrees,* and so forth; it is claimed that the classification is exhaustive and that every item of behaviour can be so classified. Such a schedule enables the investigation of a committee to be carried out by identifying specific types of problems such as that of communication, or evaluation, or control or decision-making. This analytical approach not only provides a systematic way of looking at a small group like a committee, but it enables experimental work to be carried out so that a general body of knowledge about small groups can be built up. This is what Klein (1956 and 1961) tried to do. In the second of these two books she has given verbatim records of two meetings of committees and analysed them in terms of the kind of scheme indicated above.   In considering the effectiveness of a committee we can assert that a good decision is one which is arrived at after the fullest possible exchange of information and ideas, including the members' values, and it is a decision with which all members agree.   If these conditions obtain then we may say that all the available facts have been taken into account and that morale is high.   In order for this to be so a number of functions must be performed although it is not necessary, as long as they are performed, for any person or persons to be designated formally to perform them, for responsibility lies with all the members and not merely with the chairman or leader.   The object of this kind of sociological enquiry is not merely to add to our understanding of human interaction, but on the basis of our increased knowledge of it to take steps to improve the efficiency of committees and other group activities;   no longer need the conditions which produce an effective and happy discussion group or committee be left to chance.

BIBLIOGRAPHY AND FURTHER READING

Aubert, V., and Arner, O., "On the Social Structures of the Ship", *Acta Sociologica*, Vol. 3, 1959, also in Burns, T. (Edit.) *Industrial Man*, 1969 (Penguin).

Bales, R. F., *Interaction Process Analysis*, 1951 (Addison-Wesley).

Bott, Elizabeth, *Family and Social Network: Roles, Norms and External Relationships in Ordinary Urban Families*, 1957 (Tavistock).

Davidson, H., and Lang, G., "Children's Perceptions of their Teachers", *J. Experimental Education*, 1960-1.

Festinger, L., Schachter, S., and Back, K., *Social Pressures in Informal Groups: A Study of Human Factors in Housing*, 1950 (Harper).

Goffman, E., *Asylums: Essays on the social situation of mental patients and other inmates*, 1961 (Doubleday Anchor).

Halsey, A. H., Floud, J., and Anderson, C. A. (Eds.), *Education, Economy and Society*, 1961 (Free Press).

Homans, G. G., *The Human Group*, 1951 (Routledge and Kegan Paul).

Kerr, M., *The People of Ship Street*, 1958 (Routledge and Kegan Paul).

Klein, J., *The Study of Groups*, 1956 (Routledge and Kegan Paul).
Working with Groups, 1961 (Hutchinson).
Samples from English Cultures, 1965 (Routledge and Kegan Paul).

Kuper, L., *Living in Towns*, 1953 (Cresset).

Lewin, K., Lippitt, R., and White, R. K., "Patterns of Aggressive Behaviour in Experimentally Created 'Social Climates'", *J. Soc. Psych.* Vol. X, 1939.

McGregor, O. R., *Divorce in England*, 1957 (Heinemann).

Mead, M., *Male and Female*, 1950 (Gollancz).

Mitchell, G. D., and Lupton, T., *Neighbourhood and Community*, 1954 (Liverpool University Press).

Mogey, J. M., *Family and Neighbourhood*, 1956 (O.U.P.).

Parsons, T., and Bales, R. F., *Family, Socialization and Interaction Process*, 1955 (Free Press).

Seeley, J. R., Sim, R. A., Loosley, E. W., *Crestwood Heights: A Study of the Suburban Life*, 1956 (Wiley).

Titmuss, R. M., "The Family as a Social Institution", *The Family: Report of the British National Conference on Social Work*, 1953.

Townsend, P., *The Family Life of Old People*, 1957 (Routledge and Kegan Paul).

Waller, W., *The Sociology of Teaching*, 1965 (Wiley).

Young, M., and Willmott, P., *Family and Kinship in East London*, 1957 (Routledge and Kegan Paul and Penguin).

CHAPTER X

EDUCATION: SOCIAL SYSTEM AND SOCIAL PROCESS

Why should we devote a chapter to the educational system? Would it not be more appropriate in discussing the institutions of complex societies to examine the economy instead? The economic system is, of course, a most important aspect of complex societies, and we have in fact indirectly said something about it in discussing the nature of large-scale organisation. However, in describing the nature of the educational system we shall perforce have to refer to the economy again, for it has an important bearing upon the educational arrangements of complex urban industrial societies. Yet before we do so it may be pertinent to point out that the economy is such an important part of modern complex society that in an introductory book on sociology it is necessary only to point out that discussion of it constitutes a significant department of knowledge in its own right; the subject is a specialism studied by economists; the same may be said of the political system, a subject treated by political scientists. Let it suffice to say here that the economic and political systems are both central institutional complexes of modern industrial societies and that for the present an elementary knowledge of them is assumed. We shall, therefore, devote this chapter to an examination of the educational system, an institutional complex of increasing importance and one which is closely related to both economy and government. But having said all this it is necessary to say also that education is intimately related to kinship and family as well.

Perhaps the best way to approach this subject is to make a basic distinction between the process of *socialisation* and the process of *training*. *Socialisation* begins in the family. In the simple society it is a process that is the concern, not only of the primary family group, but of the wider kinship group. In societies of the traditional kind, which we described in Part II of this book, a knowledge of kinship and family obligations is of major importance. The young must be instructed accordingly in the intricacies and complexities of kinship terminology and kinship rights and duties, but especially duties; into the nature of marriage alliances and inheritance; into succession and all other matters pertaining to descent; and into the customs and ritual practices of the tribe. By the time the child has reached puberty he or she is ready for initiation; boys especially look forward to this time, which for them possesses great social significance, when they are instructed in the final mysteries of their religion and society, and into its traditions and values; and when they have been initiated their education is complete. Of course earlier they have had opportunity to learn the skills necessary for life: in a hunting tribe the art of using bow and arrow, of trapping, and of pursuit; in an agrarian society the arts of cultivation; and among a pastoral people the arts of animal husbandry. These represent *training* but they are not elaborate technologies and so are soon learned. Thus the skills that they need are acquired without formal organisational help and with them that modicum of wisdom which enables a people to eke a living from the land, be it cultivated or wild. In this respect the educational process in the simple society differs from that in the complex type of society, for in the latter not only may training be long and difficult but education as a whole cannot be said ever to be complete, for although a formal education does come to an end it varies both in length and in content from one person to another. Let us consider this further.

Comparison of Simple and Complex Educational Systems

Modern psychological science has stressed the importance of the early years in the development of human beings. Experiences in the first few years of life have been said to lay the foundation for subsequent character building. It is not fanciful therefore to note the different ways in which infants are treated and to infer that certain consequences are likely to follow, consequences for character, temperament, and disposition; those factors which help to condition the nature of social attitudes. Thus it has been frequently noticed by anthropologists that in the simple society there is a relatively lax exercise of power or control by a mother over the infant as regards his feeding, habit-training, and general upbringing. Sometimes children are not fully habit-trained until they are well over two years of age, they tend to be fed whenever they cry rather than disciplined to eat at regular times of the day, and generally they are often irregularly attended to. This stands in contrast to the usual practice in complex societies where weaning from breast feeding is fairly rapid, where it is completed at an early age and, it may be noted, earlier than it was during the last century. Habit training is begun as soon as it is physiologically practicable. In the complex society to-day there are fewer kinsfolk available to rely on for help in child-rearing, nor is there that supply of cheap domestic labour which many people could call on fifty or sixty years ago. Moreover, there is now a widespread practice of married women continuing in some sort of employment often even when raising small children, so that the norms governing child-rearing have been accommodated to other demands made on a woman's time and energies. Moreover, when the child goes to school punctuality and regularity are prominent features of his experience. Not only may we note a greater speed in raising children through the period of infancy but we see also a differentiation in the process of training and, indeed, of socialisation as well, as the child grows. In contrast to the simple society, where traditionally a child was declared an adult on initiation, and that at the age of twelve or thirteen, we find in our own society a variety of practices which may affect some children until in their early twenties. Thus some children are selected for one kind of education and others for another kind, implying both socialisation and training of different sorts. Even if in England the "eleven plus" selection scheme has largely been abandoned there is still selection within the new comprehensive schools according to ability and aptitude and selection afterwards at the level of higher education, which is still for only a minority of young people in the population.

Thus, when we point to the contrasts between the two sorts of societies we see more clearly that the modern urban industrial society requires different things of different people. The differentiation of society on the basis of sex and age is quite insufficient, there is a differentiation according to ability, to social needs and to social stratification, and this differentiation in the educational process is of such a kind that it results in a reinforcement of the stratified system of society, albeit with modifications from time to time as the needs of society change.

The fact is that we are examining a very complex type of society, one which requires many things from its members. The parts are

162 SOCIOLOGY

not identical but different. As Durkheim put it, we are looking at an *organic* type of society in contra-distinction to the simple society which, he argued, possesses a *segmental* structure. In other words, whereas the simple society is made up of units which are identical to all intents and purposes, as one village may be like another, and one kinship group like another, the complex society is differentiated throughout. In one part there are fishing villages, in another manufacturing towns and cities, in one area we find mining communities and elsewhere spas and holiday resorts. Similarly, we must note that families differ; some are rural families, others are urban ones, some are connected with one occupation, some with another. Thus the nature of the socialisation process differs. In the professional man's family, for instance, the socialisation process differs from that of the farmer's. Here the family income may well be similar, and socialisation differs because of, as well as despite, the similarity of the familial aspirations, for in each case at least one son may be encouraged to follow a similar occupation to his father. Furthermore, the nature of the training involved, which in both cases is quite extensive, is such that a specific kind of socialisation process is necessarily associated with it. Thus a farmer's son who hopes to succeed is bound by the demands of the seasons, by the kinds of human relationships that exist, and must exist, both between the members of the farm family and between the family and others in the community. Again, a professional man's son who wishes to take up a professional career, not necessarily precisely the same as his father's, will have to be prepared for many years of study, some self-denial and postponement of immediate gratifications, and so forth. Thus in addition to undertaking a lengthy training a set of appropriate attitudes has to be learned as well. We cannot separate socialisation and training in fact, we can only do so analytically. In the complex society, unlike the simple one, the kinds of factors we have been discussing are not only pervasive but they loom large.

The Family and Education

Although most children begin life in a family, and although parental influences are primary, it is a mistake to assume that parents can rear their children as they wish. Durkheim, for one, has pointed out that parents are bound to conform to customs which if flouted take their vengeance on the children (1911, trans. 1956). He added, however, that there are as many different kinds of education as there are social *milieux* in a given society. It is useful to consider this in terms of the system of social positions that a child receives by ascription. Thus every child born into a family has a social position according to his or her sex, a position of juniority in the family as an organisation of persons, a relative position *vis à vis* any siblings, and by virtue of family membership the child is ascribed also a position in the stratified system of the society. A child requires some basic social positions from which the educational process may take its departure, and as these cannot be achieved they must be ascribed.

It must be added, however, that there is little that is innately constant about these social positions. The sex of the child may be indisputable, but the evaluations of sex, male and female, in relation to each other are variable. As Margaret Mead never tires of pointing out, it differs from one society to another, and even within any one society it may differ (1930, 1935, 1950). The age of the child alters and the relative position of age is affected by the advent of other children and the departure from the family circle of the older ones. The circumstances and the interests of the family may vary, although, broadly speaking, social class interests remain constant. In the complex society these class interests loom large in conditioning the child, in the perception and evaluation of goals, including educational goals, and thereby at least in providing differential opportunities.

The ubiquity of family life, various though its forms may be, in which the small child is an active member, would appear to reflect the prime necessity for socialising the child, or at least of providing him with some basic skills and knowledge of custom and convention so that he may acquire a respect for other people and an ability to co-operate with them in performing everyday tasks. As Davis stresses, there is a need for a society to be stable, and the socialisation of the child is the first means for ensuring this (1948, Chap. IV). Durkheim went so far as to define education as "the influence exercised by adult generations on those that are not yet ready for social life. Its object is to arouse and to develop in the child a certain number of physical, intellectual, and moral states, which are demanded of him by both the political society as a whole and the special *milieu* for which he is specifically destined" (*op. cit.*, p. 71). Whether we feel prepared to accept this definition or not, this conditioning of the infant does indeed take place. Durkheim, however, distinguished between education and pedagogy, where the latter consists of theories as to how the process of education may be consciously pursued. In Durkheim's sense of the term there is a progressive relegation of education from the family to the primary and later the secondary school. This relegation chiefly, of course, refers to the intellectual development of the child, but it may also often be seen to embrace physical and certainly moral development.

As the child grows up, more specialised agencies become responsible for his education, and at the same time a shift takes place from an emphasis on the child's ascribed positions to his achievement of positions. In the complex society, competition is institutionalised in the educational process in this way. To the child his graded position based on his attainments in class and school generally becomes more and more important, more so, that is to say, than his ascribed positions of sex, age, kinship, and social class. There is a shift, also, in the weighting of social and intellectual skills: the latter being granted an increasing importance. He is first taught basic skills such as reading, writing, and simple computation. He is then imbued with an interest in the descriptive studies of his society and the world. He is introduced to the literature of his society and then the language and literature of important and neighbouring societies. Whilst information is imparted to him there is also a progressive endeavour to discipline his mind, to teach him to be critical and reflective. He is, in other words, not merely socialised in the sense of being made to conform to customs and traditions, and to value them, but he is led to exercise his critical faculty as well. And all this takes place in a competitive atmosphere and within the framework of activities in which, for the more able child, there is a progressive postponement of immediate gratifications in the interests of long-range goals.

The Economy and Education

During the process of industrialisation in England it became increasingly obvious that the type of social structure that was emerging, with its developing technological and economic substructure, to use Marx's terms, needed a working population that was not only disciplined to the new forms and schedules of work but in addition one possessing a basic skill in reading, writing, and the ability to do simple computation.   Thus is 1871 an Education Act was passed providing for compulsory elementary education for all children; every industrialising country in its turn has been faced with the same need.   Furthermore, it later became essential for every child to have a secondary education, although the precise content of this differed from one child to another.   To be sure there have been conflicting ideological influences on this topic.   Thus some people will say that all children should have the same kind of secondary education and that in a democratic society it is unjust for it to be otherwise, whilst other people point to children's different aptitudes and abilities, and to different aspirations on the part of both children and their parents, and to the demands that a system of higher education makes on the nature of secondary education.   Be that as it may, there is no doubt that the economic system of modern society requires people to be *trained* differently and this at least to some extent must influence secondary educational curricula.   If the tripartite scheme of grammar, technical, and modern secondary education is disappearing, it nevertheless remains true that for those children who are to go on to university a more academic type of course is necessary than for those who are not, and that those who intend to acquire technical and manual skills need a training of a somewhat different sort.   And it also remains true that the needs of the economy will largely dictate the proportions undertaking different kinds of training, whatever the arrangements made for that training may be.   If it is held that in modern society every child has a social right to receive that education which suits his character and abilities then it follows that it is the task of government to reconcile these aspirations with the needs of the economy.   From the sociologist's point of view, however, the task is to assess the extent to which the educational system does provide equality of opportunity so that the first of these considerations may be fulfilled and to assess the extent to which changes in the economy are reflected in the provision for education.   In recent years an increasing interest in these topics has been taken by sociologists, especially by those in Britain.

In all industrialised societies there is a process of change stemming from technological innovations and this is primarily seen in the development of the economy; the current interest in automation is merely a recognition of one important stage in this process. Technological innovations alter the nature of the work task, they bring about new tasks and new grouping of work activity. Thus we see a host of new occupations, many of which acquire semi-professional status in the community; this is most noticeable among the medical auxiliaries like radiographers, physiotherapists, and dieticians, but we see it also in other spheres as, for instance, computer programmers come into existence in commerce and government, and all kinds of technicians in chemical engineering, agricultural science, and space travel. Education has ceased to be divided sharply into primary education for all and a special education for an élite. Thus reforms in secondary, higher, and further education have greatly altered the educational system. It is not so much the case that more education has to be vocational as that certain kinds of attitudes have to be acquired and aptitudes cultivated so as to enable men and women to draw on general principles for guidance in the application of technological knowledge in a wide variety of fields. Such knowledge has also to be applied in the sphere of administration as well as in factory and workshop activities. Thus branch banking to-day, for example, is a very different kind of activity from what it was a decade or two ago, for bank clerks have different kinds of tasks to perform as new forms of mechanical equipment are introduced and as rationalisation proceeds, and so it is for other kinds of business activity. Much of the new training required is carried out in the firms and organisations concerned, with short courses of instruction interspersed with practical experience. Sometimes employees are seconded or released for special training in other organisations and in Technical Institutes. Thus the picture of the educational system has become very complex and varied; not all education, nor the training aspect of it which is what we are considering in particular, is confined to schools and colleges, nor is it full-time or continuous.

One consequence of these larger demands which the economy makes on the educational system is the desire to utilise human resources to greater advantage. Thus the waste of the old system is being removed and increasing endeavours are being made not only to provide an education which people can profit from according to their ability and aptitude, but to investigate the reasons why those with innate capacity fail to make the best use of opportunities provided. Indeed, the importance of ensuring equality of opportunity has stimulated sociologists to carry out investigations to measure the extent of existing inequalities of opportunity and to isolate the factors responsible for the state of affairs where opportunity is provided but is not taken.

Equality of Educational Opportunity

The American sociologist Ralph Turner (see Halsey, *et. al.* 1961) has pointed to a distinction between ways of promoting educational mobility, that is to say mobility from primary to secondary and from secondary to higher education. Thus he contrasts *sponsored* and *contest* mobility. In the former case children are selected by teachers or by examination processes so that a proportion are permitted to proceed to a higher form of education. In Britain, since the 1944 Education Act this was a selection at eleven years of age or over from among primary school pupils for either a secondary grammar or a secondary modern schooling, the former of these two being educationally advantageous, and again, a later selection from grammar schools for university and college education. In the case of contest mobility all children receive the same type of secondary education and although there may be hurdles for them to jump they can make repeated attempts to surmount them. Thus in the U.S.A., for example, a person may gain admittance to a state university or college fairly easily and will have repeated opportunity to pass qualifying examinations or tests in order to graduate. The differences between these two types of mobility originate in different value systems, but essentially it means that in sponsored mobility there is selection at an early age with specific and distinctive educational treatment in schools and universities designed for the purpose of producing an élite, and in contest mobility there is a reduction in the sharpness of the separation of people of different levels of ability in the schools. Thus, for example, the comprehensive high school is universal in the U.S.A. and there is easy access to higher education. Thus many have the opportunity to embark on it even though there is a high failure rate afterwards. Yet we should observe that failures may try again, or may move to another college with less exacting standards. Failure there may be, but it need not be final.

In England during the 1950s an increasing criticism of the values underlying sponsored mobility was voiced. This criticism stemmed partly from the attraction of egalitarian ideals and partly from the changing needs of the British economy which we referred to earlier. One study proved to be very influential. It was part of a series of investigations carried out by the Department of Sociological and Demographical Research of the London School of Economics and Political Science, which we referred to in Chapter VII; the study took place in 1952, the results being published by Floud, Halsey, and Martin (1956). This investigation was limited to a comparison of two areas in England, namely south-west Hertfordshire and Middlesbrough. The former is a fairly prosperous suburban area near London, the latter is in the industrial north. Whilst they offer marked contrasts, neither is an unrepresentative area, either structurally or historically. The investigators were especially interested in the social origins of boys entering secondary grammar schools, which provide the major recruiting grounds for higher education. They concentrated their attention on the occupational background of fathers, dividing them broadly into middle, lower middle, and working classes.

The first social class included professional people, business owners, and managers, the second included clerical workers, foremen, small shopkeepers, etc., and the third included skilled and unskilled manual workers. They show that whilst the proportion of boys with working-class background in pre-war years was 16 per cent. in Hertfordshire and 46 per cent. in Middlesbrough, it had risen after the war to 25 per cent. and 52 per cent. respectively, and that most of the increase was associated with skilled manual workers. Since the passing of the Education Act of 1944 the proportion of working-class boys in Hertfordshire had increased to about 40 per cent., whilst in Middlesbrough it had remained fairly constant. In Hertfordshire this increase had been at the expense of the lower middle class. Notwithstanding these facts, it remains the case that the chances of a working-class boy reaching a grammar school are not much different from what they were before the Act was implemented in 1945.

Opportunity, however, must be related to ability. Measured

intelligence was the only indicator available for estimating ability. On this basis the investigators discovered that in Middlesbrough a rough equality of opportunity had existed since the 1920s, but in south-west Hertfordshire many able working-class boys had been excluded from grammar school education before 1945, but that since that time the same equality of opportunity had existed as obtained in Middlesbrough.

The fact is that there is an unequal distribution of measured intelligence, and this is because it is partly an acquired characteristic.* It is not easy, however, to determine the social and environmental factors conditioning it.   There is some evidence that on the average children from large families score less well on intelligence tests than those from small families.   The material conditions of children's homes seem to have some bearing on their success, but not so much as size of family.   A further factor of importance is the parental attitudes.   Indeed, the attitudes and ambitions of parents were reflected in the performance of children in examinations in all classes.   As the investigators point out, the percentage of parents of both sexes who received grammar school education and some further education was twice as high among the successful as among the unsuccessful in south-west Hertfordshire and three times as high in Middlesbrough.   Frequently, mothers prior to marriage had had an occupation superior to that of their husbands.

It would seem that the education, attitudes, and ambitions of parents play a large part in conditioning children.   This is hardly surprising, for the primary group of the family is powerful in introjecting goals and instilling habits and attitudes.   The educated parent clearly possesses an advantage in his knowledge of the educational system, the different opportunities open to children who have passed through grammar or technical schools.   But the subtleties of this family influence go far beyond just this, and of their nature we can as yet say little.   But what we may say is that the ascription of social class positions is a fundamental factor in determining the child's opportunities, not so much to-day because one class is economically in a better situation than another to secure

* According to P. E. Vernon (1958) and Sir Cyril Burt (1959), 20 per cent. of the differences in measured intelligence in primary school children may be the result of environmental factors.

these opportunities, although this is still true, but because parents tend to differ according to social class in their attitudes; they hold out different goals before their children, they give them different degrees of encouragement, and they present them with different examples of adult behaviour and interests. Education begins and is continued in the family, and some children are educated better than others in the appreciation of the value of education.

The British Government has in recent years sponsored a number of research projects to assess the social factors affecting educational performance and investigations have also been carried out by Royal Commissions and by Departmental Committees. Among these, the Crowther Report of 1959, the Newsom and the Robbins Reports of 1963, and the Plowden Report of 1967 may be said to be landmarks. An excellent summary of these and the researches undertaken in connection with the policy matters they refer to has been made by Olive Banks (1968).

Education and Change

We began by making a distinction between socialisation and training, indicating that education includes both. It should be evident that socialisation is essentially a matter of transmitting values and attitudes from old to young, and as such that it tends to be inimical to change. But education is also concerned to instil critical attitudes as well. In democratic societies this critical element is valued for its own sake, and this too is transmitted. However, it may be held that it can only be so provided there is a certain degree of autonomy in the educational system. There are two spheres where we may find this. One is in the teaching profession and the other is in the independence of parts of the educational system from other institutional complexes, especially government. Of course the two are not unconnected. In England the role of the teacher has been on the whole valued rather less than in other European countries, although a possible exception may be the staffs of the Public Schools. Tropp (1956) in his history of the teaching profession traces the vicissitudes in the profession's fate, the sources of recruitment, and the nature of remuneration. Brookover and Gottlieb (1955) discussing the profession in America also point to its differentiated character and the variety of sources of employment. As a profession, teachers are less united than the members of the medical and legal professions, and are felt to be inferior to them in status. In so far as the state employs most teachers they are not free to set their own standards of entry or performance, which are hallmarks of a profession. Hitherto, an exception has been the smaller body of University teachers, but then the Universities have enjoyed a degree of academic freedom which has been maintained despite increasing state control, although how long this will continue is uncertain. Here we may find that degree of autonomy which enables critical attitudes to be formed and encouraged. Yet it is easy to exaggerate this feature and it must be allowed that in many countries schools and universities have been used as a means of instilling the official ideology, and independent thought related to values rather than to technology has been discouraged. A country may depend on its educational system for both socialisation and training, but unless a vigorous tradition of critical enquiry is also encouraged education may systematically be brought into the service of the state rather than enhanced in value for the benefit of the people.

BIBLIOGRAPHY AND FURTHER READING

Banks, Olive, *The Sociology of Education*, 1968 (Batsford).

Brookover, W. A., and Gottlieb, D., *A Sociology of Education*, 1955 (American Book Company).

Burt, C., "General Ability and Special Aptitudes", *Educ. Research.* Vol. 1, No. 2, 1959.

Carr-Saunders, A. M., and Wilson, P. A., *The Professions*, 1933 (Clarendon Press).

Davis, K., *Human Society*, 1948 (The Macmillan Co.).

Durkheim, E., *Education and Sociology*, 1911, *trans*. 1956 (Free Press).
   Professional Ethics and Civil Morals, 1957 (Routledge and Kegan Paul).

Floud, J. E., Halsey, A. H., and Martin, F. M., *Social Class and Educational Opportunity*, 1956 (Heinemann).

Halsey, A. H., Floud, J., and Anderson, C. A., Eds., *Education, Economy and Society: A Reader in the Sociology of Education*, 1961 (Free Press).

Mays, J. B., *Education and the Urban Child*, 1962 (Liverpool University Press).

Mead, M., *Growing up in New Guinea*, 1930, 1954 (Pelican).
 Sex and Temperament in Three Primitive Societies, 1935 (Routledge).
 Male and Female, 1950 (Gollancz).

Musgrave, P. W., *The Sociology of Education*, 1965 (Methuen).

Spindler, G. D., *Education and Culture*, 1963 (Holt, Rinehart, and Winston).

Taylor, W., *The Secondary Modern School*, 1963 (Faber).

Tropp, A., *The School Teachers*, 1956 (Heinemann).

Vernon, P. E., "A New Look at Intelligence Testing", *Educ. Research*, Vol. 1, No. 1, 1958.

CONCLUSIONS

What has gone before has been by nature of an introduction. What has been introduced is a way of thinking about human society. It is not the only way and it is unlikely to continue for long unchanged, for knowledge grows and our ways of thinking either develop or perish. Sociology will develop because new problems arise which demand new and more effective ways of thinking and because the methods hitherto advocated prove to be inadequate.

Clearly, there are limits to what can be accomplished by sociologists. In this presentation of the subject we have severely limited ourselves. No mention, for instance, has been made of the influence exerted by men and women of strong character and intelligence on their environment, and people do succeed from time to time in leaving their own individual and unique mark on society. Indeed, this is a topic that Miss Emmet considered in her important book, *Function, Purpose, and Powers*, and it led her to consider besides functions both purposes and vocations.

Again, society is not static, and we have been apt to assume that it is; moreover, man is curious and questioning, whereas we have assumed him to be unreflective. Whilst we may profitably, for certain purposes, assume the ubiquity of routine and unreflectiveness in mankind, sufficient to enable us to pursue a functional analysis, we should know we are making these assumptions, and know also that some time we shall have to ask just how far they are reasonable, and seek to learn what we shall have to do in modifying our scheme of thought to permit more realistic assumptions. A failure to re-examine these assumptions will justly call forth a rebuke from those who experience a call to determine events and who possess the imagination to create new forms of social life.

Besides the problems which arise in considering the theoretical status of our discipline there are its practical implications. What, we may be asked, at the present stage of its development has sociology to offer? We have suggested throughout that sociology has a bearing on administration. It has also something to contribute to aid the social worker and the teacher. What is the nature

173

of this contribution? There are some obvious answers. We might say that sociology can present the social worker with some facts about society and may do so with some degree of precision. It may estimate, for example, the extent of poverty, defined in some agreed manner, and indeed point to the incidence of poverty among various sections of the population. Or it may, by an examination of the relationships between kin in various sections of the population, estimate the differential needs of the aged. To the teacher it can give information about our society, the factors conditioning the personalities of children from different social *milieux*, rural and urban, middle and working class, and so forth. It may even provide the information which he deems necessary to impart to children so that they may be better informed about their own society and others.

But perhaps we may point to something more than this. The teacher and the social worker are practical people. They are engaged in practising an art. They bring to their tasks qualtities of personality and character, but they also appeal to principles. These principles are derived from knowledge lending itself to application. As they are concerned with people this knowledge may be said to be embraced by applied social science. Now, one cannot apply particular knowledge to any great extent, for particular knowledge is of limited value and is restricted in scope. The principles appealed to are drawn from generalised knowledge, and this means that behind the principles are organised bodies of generalised knowledge; this is supplied by the theoretical social disciplines. Sociology, as we have defined it, is a descriptive and analytical discipline which seeks through the use of the comparative method to generalise; to this extent it is a theoretical discipline. Hence, just as the medical practitioner derives principles of treatment from medical science, so his medical science is informed by the descriptive, analytical, and theoretical sciences of anatomy, physiology, pathology, and so forth. It is the same in the social sciences. The qualified generalisations of sociology, together with those of psychology, are of direct interest to the social worker and the teacher. They are also, together with economics, of relevance to the policy-maker and administrator.

What has sociology to offer at present? In the first place, it enables us to appreciate the variety in forms of social life. If the study of the simpler societies has done nothing else it has certainly achieved this, and perhaps in the process rendered us more humble in the face of the richness of custom and practice. It has shown us that there is often more than one way of arranging human relationships to achieve man's ends. It has demonstrated the important truth that forms of social behaviour seemingly disparate and even oddly unique may be closely connected.

These lessons learned we may turn to study the more complex society, which we think we are familiar with, and be more ready to learn from other people so as to help us reduce the otherwise unanticipated consequences of social action. To discern not only the manifest but also the latent functions of institutionalised forms of behaviour is perhaps the prime task of the sociologist. This discernment is essential to policy-making and administration.

In a society that increases in complexity it will not do to assume that our major social problems are merely the simple effects of simple causes. Whether we are concerned with colonial administration, medical, social, or religious work among strange peoples, the settlement of West Indians in our industrial cities, slum clearance and re-housing, urban and rural development, changing production methods in industry, or the efficiency of social organisations, we may find in the kind of analysis briefly outlined in this introduction something of direct relevance.

Politics, and the word is used here in its broadest sense, is the art of the possible. Sociology, among other social disciplines, helps us to understand the scope and the limits of what is possible and the implications of possible action. It cannot determine the ends, except in the sense of describing the ends that people do in fact pursue, but it may enable us to say something about the means in relation to given ends, and this, together with the belief that curiosity is not without its own intrinsic value, must be our justification for pursuing the study of social systems.

INDEX OF SUBJECTS

176

INDEX OF NAMES

178

PRINTED IN GREAT BRITAIN BY UNIVERSITY TUTORIAL PRESS LTD, FOXTON
NEAR CAMBRIDGE